BURDEN SHARING IN NATO

Burden Sharing
in NATO

Gavin Kennedy

HM

Holmes & Meier Publishers, Inc.
New York

First published in the United States of America 1979 by
Holmes & Meier Publishers, Inc.
30 Irving Place, New York, N.Y. 10003

Copyright © 1979 Gavin Kennedy

Library of Congress Cataloging in Publication Data

Kennedy, Gavin.
  Burden sharing in NATO.
  Bibliography: p.
  Includes index.
  1. North Atlantic Treaty Organization—Finance.
I. Title.
UA646.3.K39   1979   355.03'1'091821   79–12140
ISBN 0–8419–0515–0

Printed in Great Britain

Contents

Preface

This book was researched during my tenure as a NATO Research Fellow in 1977 and I am grateful to NATO for the opportunity that its financial support gave me to travel within NATO countries. Of course, none of the views expressed can be attributed in any way to individuals in that organisation nor to the representatives of the member states.

I acknowledge the support and assistance of Fernand Welter, Head of Education and Cultural Relations at NATO Headquarters, Brussels, David Greenwood, Director of Defence Studies at the University of Aberdeen and Professor Alan Tait, formerly Head of Department at the University of Strathclyde and presently Head of Fiscal Studies at the International Monetary Fund, Washington. Other persons greatly assisted me in the research and discussion but must remain anonymous, due to their civil service or military occupations.

I have made much use of the work of the international academic community and hope that my interpretations have done justice to the originality of those quoted in the text. Numerous students have also contributed to my selection of content and presentation.

Defence economics is a fascinating subject as long as we always remember that we study defence in order to live in peace.

University of Strathclyde   G.K.
January 1979

For the Officers and Men of the Scottish Regiments

Introduction

This book is about the economics of military alliance. In particular it is about burden or cost sharing. It therefore combines a review of the economic theory of collective action and a study of the actual, and potential, arrangements for burden sharing in an existing military alliance, the North Atlantic Treaty Organisation (NATO).

It should be made clear at the outset that this is not a history of NATO nor a forecast of how things might develop in NATO over the next decade. Much of the discussion refers directly to NATO by way of example, but many of the conclusions could apply to other international organisations. The growth and proliferation of international organisations in recent years is worthy of a study in itself. What these organisations have in common is the need to devise a method of allocating their costs among their members. The discussion of the available alternatives for funding is central to the main theme of this book.

How should the costs of an international organisation be divided among its members? What criteria might be used to determine each participant's contribution? What effect does relative wealth disparity have on members' ability to pay? Should those who benefit most pay the most, and if so how do we identify the beneficiaries? What happens if members will not pay their share?

These questions are of interest to both economists and policy makers. They also raise sensitive issues of equity and fairness. Neither at the international nor at the national level (where these issues are replicated in the distribution of costs among tax payers for public services) has it been necessary to postpone working arrangements for funding collective activities until unanimity is reached among members. The extent and ingenuity of the payment systems in use throughout the national states and various international organisations provide a wealth of useful experience for this discussion.

Interest in international cost sharing is likely to grow rather than diminish. The number of international organisations continues to increase and the number of international programmes associated with these organisations is also increasing. In the United Nations, agency programmes are expanding all the time, for example in the Food and Agriculture Organisation (FAO), but also in the international peace-keeping forces such as in the Middle East. The proposals for a New International Economic Order involve complex cost-sharing arrangements between suppliers and consumers of certain key commodities. The wide disparity in per capita incomes between countries adds to the problems of equity, and while this is in sharpest relief in the case of the developing primary producers and the industrialised primary consumers it nevertheless is of importance when considering payments between industrialised countries which also have relative disparities in their per capita incomes.

No general solution of the cost-sharing problem has yet been devised. In its place there are a number of partial, or expedient, solutions which are used by the various agencies. In some cases the solution leans towards a benefit approach, where benefits can be identified and where those members that appear to benefit most are also the members with relatively high incomes. In other cases the solution leans towards an ability-to-pay approach where who benefits is less important than who can afford to pay. Not surprisingly, it is not unusual to find cost-sharing arrangements that combine elements of both approaches. The criterion of ability to pay (normally per capita GDP) is weighted by some indicator of benefit (who gains?) or, increasingly more commonly, by some indicator of interest (which is not necessarily the same thing as benefit). For example, in a commodity agreement a low per capita GDP country may benefit from the agreement (higher regular prices for its exports) while a high per capita GDP country has an interest in the agreement working because of felt obligations to

Third World development.

A military alliance presents some interesting aspects of international cost sharing. An alliance may simply involve a stated (even secret) commitment to aid an alliance member if a third party attacks it. For all other intents and purposes the members would act independently of each other and there would be no association of the military forces of each country. The level of military preparedness of any member would be a purely national matter and of no concern to its allies. In these circumstances cost sharing would be of minimal interest to the members as common costs would be negligible, if not zero.

In this study we are more concerned with a military alliance that involves a much greater (and open) degree of commitment by the members. They are not just pledged to assist each other in the event of a military attack. There is a relatively high degree of integration of the national defence forces and a correspondingly higher visible cost of collective services. The national defence forces can be placed under alliance command (in NATO in Europe the forces come under the Supreme Allied Commander Europe—SACEUR). The supranational nature of alliance military authority proved unacceptable to the French and they have withdrawn their forces from this arrangement. However, the majority of the NATO members have accepted supranational authority, though it must be noted that this authority is carefully controlled politically.

A military alliance with partially integrated defence forces has two elements to it: those common costs that are incurred by the alliance on behalf of the members, and those national costs that are incurred by the individual members primarily on their own account and only indirectly on behalf of the alliance. The former costs are relatively small compared with the latter. It is no accident that cost-sharing arrangements for the common costs have been negotiated according to a guideline formula, but absolutely no progress has been made on a formula for sharing out the national costs even where the national contributions of some members are regarded as being of central importance to the effectiveness of the alliance. The major stumbling block to a burden-sharing agreement is the sheer magnitude of the sums involved—there would be no point in re-allocating the burden among members unless substantial changes were made, and it is not politically possible to make substantial changes without threatening the cohesion of the alliance.

It might justly be asked, if substantial change is not possible why bother discussing the topic at all? The obvious reason is that the topic will not go away just because it is not discussed. Secondly, the topic of cost sharing is of increasing interest in related fields of international co-operation. Thirdly, practical experience in other fields and developments in alliance economics suggest that new arrangements can be devised that are worthy of consideration. Fourthly, informed discussion is of better value than blind faith and ignorance, even if both methods lead to the same conclusion. The discussion on alliance cost sharing in this book is a contribution to a wider discussion, and the economic theory outlined in the following chapters will prove beneficial in those wider discussions. It will, it is hoped, prove beneficial to the discussion within the military alliance as well.

1

Public Goods and Collective Action

The economic theory of military alliance is based on a number of related concepts. These include the theory of public goods, so-called 'free riding', market failure, the theory of collective action, small member exploitation of larger members, topics from micro-economic theory (marginal costs, marginal rates of substitution, indifference curves, Edgeworth Box diagrams, etc.) and the transfer problem. In this and the next chapter I will discuss and introduce some of these concepts. The discussion will necessarily be a summary one, but references are given for further study. The material forms a foundation for a critical review of alliance theory.

Private and public goods

A private good has two characteristics which are essential for the market to act as an efficient allocator of resources: exclusion and rivalry. An inability to pay the supplier, for whatever reason, necessarily excludes the consumer from acquiring a private good; the purchase of a private good necessarily reduces the amount of that good available to all other individuals. Explicitly, a private good X_n can be divided among different individuals $(1, 2, \ldots i, \ldots s)$ so that:

$$X_n = \sum_1^s X_j^i$$

In words, the sum of the amounts of good X_n divided among different consumers is equal to the total amount of the good available. If a single individual bought the total amount of X_n available, there would be none left for others. Each amount of the good bought reduces the amount available for others.

A public good is the polar opposite of the private good—it is non-exclusive and non-rival. No individual's consumption of the public good precludes any other individual's consumption of that good up to the full amount provided. The amount of a public good X_m available to one consumer is simultaneously available to all other consumers:

$$X_m^1 = X_m \quad \text{and} \quad X_m^2 = X_m$$

Individual consumers of a public good are non-rival in consumption (Samuelson 1954, 1955). Moreover, they cannot be excluded from consumption once the good is provided. If they cannot be excluded they cannot be charged and if they cannot be charged the good cannot be provided by a market.

A market depends on consumers revealing their preferences by paying for the goods they wish to consume. By revealing their preferences consumers signal to producers their preferred output mix. If the consumers cannot, or will not, provide signals for the market it cannot respond to their preferences.

Why would a consumer rationally fail to signal a preference for a public good? The answer goes to the heart of the public good problem. For each individual the provision of a public good is an invitation to consume the full amount available. This invitation is open to the individual whether or not he contributes to the cost of provision. If he does not contribute, and the public good is still provided, there is no way to prevent him consuming the good. Thus for each individual there is no incentive (other than a superior sense of moral duty) to reveal a preference for the public good. In the absence of an incentive there is a presumption that they will be shy of revealing their preferences. If they do so and the public good is provided by the contributions of others they can still enjoy the benefits of consuming the good—they become free riders.

An alternative to a market has to be found if public goods are to be provided. The alternative can be an analogue for a market, such as a voting system. It could be a welfare injunction operated through some omnipresent being.

Markets and public goods

Adam Smith noted that there were some activities which it would not pay an individual, or group of individuals, to undertake as a commercial venture but which, if undertaken, would be of benefit to society. He suggested that the state should finance such undertakings (Smith 1776, book V, ch. 1). This is a recognition of the possibility of market failure by an economist closely identified with the idea of free markets.

A public good is characterised by its properties of non-exclusion and non-rivalry and not by the mode of its provision. Public goods can be provided privately and private goods can be provided publicly. Hence, the existence of the possibility of a public good is not necessarily a presumption in favour of state provision. Once a common goal or interest is provided a public good has been created for the members of the group concerned (Olson 1965).

Market failure (Smith's example) might imply the state taking on the task of providing a good or service. A common interest (Olson's example) might imply a group of people using the market to provide themselves with a public good.

There is no difficulty in assigning the provision of pure private goods to the market, assuming that the distribution of income in society is tolerable. A perfectly competitive economy could be disgusting on ethical grounds—so could a perfectly egalitarian economy that is run by megalomaniacs. For purposes of this discussion we allow that a market economy will approximate as an efficient, and tolerable, allocative mechanism.

There is a continuum of types of goods between the polar cases of pure private and pure public goods. The same good can have different characteristics in different settings and at different times for different people. This has particular relevance for national defence which has the characteristics of a pure public good in one circumstance (deterrence) but may only be a partial public good in other circumstances (actual war).

Four main cases can be identified (Musgrave & Musgrave 1976, p. 52; Peston 1972). The pure private good which is exclusive and rival and the pure public good which is non-exclusive and non-rival are the two polar cases. In between there are two cases: a good which is exclusive but non-rival and a good which is rival and non-exclusive.

A bridge is an example of a good which is non-rival (at least up to capacity) but open to exclusion. A vehicle using the bridge does not consume the bridge's services in rivalry with other vehicles—many vehicles can use the services of bridges without interfering with each other at any level of usage below capacity (at and above capacity congestion occurs and consumption is then rival). It is possible to exclude potential users of the bridge's services by means of toll charges. Those drivers that do not pay the toll can be prevented from crossing the bridge.

Should a toll be imposed on bridges (or any other part of the road system)? This raises normative issues. On the grounds that it is possible to identify those who benefit from the bridge it can be argued that they should be charged. The level of the toll can be set to recover construction costs, thus providing funds for further public provision or reductions in taxation. The toll can be set to recover the operating cost of the bridge alone (including the cost of collection of the tolls). This would reduce the amount of public expenditure that would otherwise be required for maintenance. On the other hand it can be argued that the marginal cost of consuming the bridge's services once it is provided is near or about zero (depending on maintenance costs) and that it is therefore sub-optimal to charge vehicles for use. As a charge will reduce use at the margin, it is inefficient to impose one while use is non-rival.

Another example of a case of non-rivalry in consumption where exclusion is feasible is that of radio and television reception. The number of receivers does not affect the strength of the signal and consequently consumption is non-rival (assuming that the receivers are not adjacent). Exclusion is possible through the use of scrambling devices which make reception available only to those who pay for the unscrambling device. The market can be used to allocate the costs of transmission to listeners or viewers. Should it be used for this purpose, or should some other means be found to pay for transmission and programme costs, such as advertising or licence fees? Arguments can be used in support of various alternative schemes but the main point for us is that the possibility of exclusion is not an economic justification for it.

A good can be rival but non-exclusive. Urban roads, for example, are often congested with vehicular traffic. Consumption is rival in that each person's use of road space inhibits the free movement of other vehicles. The space occupied by a private car cannot be used by the bus behind it. Exclusion, through making those who use the road space at congested times pay for the privilege, is for all practical purposes not possible at present (though some disagree, e.g. Roth 1967). The expense of monitoring and identifying road users (with current technology) probably exceeds the benefits of road rationing.

The case is clearer in the example of an orchard next to a garden with bee hives in it. From the bee's point of view there is rivalry: what one bee gets from a flower or blossom cannot be taken by another bee from another hive. Yet how can the bees be excluded either by the inhabitants of one hive at the expense of another, or by the owner of the orchard who might prefer his own bees to have a monopoly of the blossom? Exclusion would be inordinately expensive.

How goods should be provided is a question that involves a normative approach. Whether the market provides them or not will depend on ethical values, administrative convenience, politics and the importance of efficiency. Markets are successful allocators of resources in certain circumstances and not so successful in others. The market and the public sector need not be mutually exclusive, and have operated side by side throughout history. The state can buy what the market produces and distribute it according to some ethical criterion of fairness. It can also pay the market to provide goods for the community according to some ethical criterion of need. The state can also produce the goods itself and sell them to the community as part of the market or distribute them outside the market. There is no presumption in favour of total state provision, and experience suggests that there are substantial diseconomies in total state monopoly.

Collective action

I have already referred to Olson's view that 'the achievement of any common goal or the satisfaction of any common interest means that a public or collective good has been provided for that group' (Olson 1965, p. 15). This has important implications for the theory of public goods.

What motivates people to join common interest groups? The answer is not at all obvious. If a common interest group is formed to provide a public good there is an incentive for individual free riding. Organisations serve collective interests, not individual interests. Individual interests are best served by individual actions, but collective interests can only be served by collective action. Hence individuals who join an organisation to serve a collective interest will sacrifice some part of their individual interests by doing so. It is not obvious that collective interests are preferable to individual interests and therefore some form of persuasion must take place if individuals are to join an organisation. This persuasion can take one of two forms (and sometimes a mixture of both): inducement or coercion.

Inducement can take the form of offering prospective members a benefit in addition to the collective goal of the organisation. This compensates the individual for the sacrifice of some of his individual benefits.

Trade unions provide an example of persuasion by inducement. Most unions offer their members benefits separate from their collective bargaining activity, such as (in Britain) access to higher education (scholarships to Ruskin College in Oxford, the London School of Economics and the Open University), discount purchasing privileges with traders, low cost holidays in communist countries, convalescence homes, sickness and death benefits, social clubs, legal aid and extensive access to important public institutions either to influence them (lobbying) or to participate in them (union sponsorship to become an MP, local councillor, Justice of the Peace, member of the public authority, etc.). Other inducements by organisations can be found in golf clubs (the members' 19th hole), residents' associations (the childrens' Christmas party), professional organisations (reduced conference fees, discounts on books, equipment and general supplies) and in students' unions (discount rail travel, etc.)

Coercion is also common. The state does not rely on a citizen's sense of patriotism to induce a voluntary payment for the costs of provision of public services. If it did the sum of voluntary contributions would likely fall far short of the costs even when the citizens voted unanimously for a specific service to be provided. Hence taxation is levied by law, with penalties for non-compliance. Likewise, trade unions also use coercion to gain members through Union Membership Agreements, or the closed shop.

Persuasion is necessary because of the conflict between individual and collective interests. Sometimes the amount of persuasion available is not enough to obtain the desired result. For economic theory we take the example of the perfectly competitive industry which, if it could restrict its output, could raise its price—the demand curve for the industry is downward sloping. The individual firm in the perfectly competitive industry seeks to maximise its output at the going industry price at the level where marginal cost equals marginal revenue. If all the firms in the industry behave this way, which the model asserts they will, the output of the industry cannot be restricted. As long as this is the case collective interests (higher prices and higher profits) are in conflict with individual interests (output maximisation and normal profits).

The Organisation of Petroleum Exporting Countries (OPEC) is a cartel of individual national producers who have a relatively homogeneous product in conditions of (short run) price inelasticity of demand. If, before 1973, an individual supplier had raised prices by even a small amount, he would have risked an output increase by competitors at the current lower price. Only when they all agreed to raise prices simultaneously and restrict output was it possible for the market price to rise so dramatically. The benefits of this new higher price are open to all petroleum producers whether they are in OPEC or not. Britain, since 1974, has become an oil producer from its fields in the North Sea off the coast of Scotland. The price of British oil is the same as the OPEC price, though Britain is not a member. By not joining OPEC Britain is excluded from the price fixing discussions though she naturally gains from the maintained high prices agreed by the members. Britain does not have to contribute to the costs of running OPEC, nor is she compelled to suffer any opprobrium directed at the OPEC producers by consumers. Britain free rides on the OPEC cartel with a bonus of diplomatic advantage—a classic case of individual interest being in conflict with group interest.

In similar vein individuals join a trade union to further group interests as nations might join a cartel. An individual who engaged in output restriction (an individual strike) would be replaced by the management. The rewards to individuals in a firm are rival and exclusive when they are in the form of discretionary payments, promotion and better jobs. But in a group the rewards take the form of a public good. Collective output restriction (a group strike) can raise the price of labour services. To ensure compliance with group restrictions there is a need for coercion to maintain group solidarity. This fact itself supports the contention that group interests are in conflict with individual interests.

In both the above examples the public good provided by collective action is in the form of a higher price for what the group supplies. There are costs involved in providing that public good, and these costs need not be trivial. The secretariat expenses of OPEC are quite small compared to the value of the product the members sell on world markets, but there are other potential costs of much greater magnitude. A cartel may provoke retaliation—even military intervention, as mooted by Dr Kissinger's office following the 1973 price hike. Employee strikes can be, and sometimes are, bitterly contested by the employers and impose substantial costs on the individuals who participate in them. It would be wrong to see conflicts of this nature bounded by a calculus of costs and benefits but there is evidence that the costs of enforcing an output restriction programme contribute in some measure to the caution which individuals, and governments, bring to a decision to participate, or promote, militant action in support of a common objective.

The wider use of the concept of public goods is helpful for much of the discussion that follows. The degrees of rivalry and exclusion which some public goods can possess in different circumstances are of direct relevance in cases of military alliance.

Defence as a public good

So far pure public goods have been discussed without any specific examples of them being identified. The characteristics of the polar case of the pure public good—non-exclusion and non-rivalry—are all that has been necessary so far for the discussion to take place. It is appropriate now, however, to discuss specific goods that might come within the definition of public goods.

The usual textbook examples are lighthouses (but see Coase 1974), law and order, national defence and (following Samuelson 1955) outdoor circuses. On the latter I have no comment to make, except to note Samuelson's affinity with Olson on the wider concept of public goods. My interest in this concluding section of the chapter is in national defence as a public good.

Why is national defence regarded as a pure public good? The simple explanation is that once national defence is provided all the citizens of the nation are defended equally—'everyone receives a full share of protection from the military machine' (Margolis 1954). This is fine as a working definition but it must be subject to some qualifications if greater precision is sought.

The attractions of the simple working definition are obvious. Teachers can illustrate a lecture on pure public goods with a recognisable example. The nature of *national* defence—mass protection of all the citizens within and beyond the national territory—lends itself to use as an illustration of non-exclusion. It would be extremely costly, not to say administratively inconvenient, for the defence forces to be selective about who or what they defended. The idea of selective defence runs counter to the normal principles of national sovereignty.

The benefits of national defence are externalised and the

consumption of those benefits by one citizen does not in any way reduce the amount of defence available to any other citizen. Defence is therefore non-rival (Kennedy 1975). Hence for teachers it is an ideal example.

In addition, it is useful as an illustration of the possibility of free riding. Once national defence is provided everybody in the community is protected and none can efficiently be excluded. If the payment for defence was based on the voluntary contributions of the citizens the amount received by the government would likely fall far short of the expenditures made. Each individual would have an incentive to mislead the authorities regarding his or her preference for defence. If they are excused payments they certainly cannot be excluded from the benefits.

It would not be easy to distinguish between those who genuinely prefer not to be defended (pacifists) and those who are deliberately free riding (non-pacifists who want somebody else to pay for their defence), nor would it be easy to cope with those who support the invasion of their own country because of some affinity they feel with the enemy. None of these groups will want to contribute to national defence if they can avoid it. Meade's (1973) tongue-in-cheek suggestion that the citizens meet and decide on a voluntary subscription from those who want defence plus a sum for compensating those who do not obviously falls down on the impossibility of exclusion.

National defence as an instrument of deterrence can be estimated as a probability of non-attack. If deterrence succeeds—no attack takes place—unambiguously everybody benefits (except those who wanted an attack). This is a case of a pure public good. But this is not necessarily the case if deterrence breaks down.

The situation is analagous to that of congestion on a public road. The community gains from having a road but when congestion occurs it can hardly be argued that one motorist's consumption of the road has no effect on another's. Similarly, in an attack on the territory of a country the consumption of defence resources by one sector could conceivably be at the expense of another sector's. Some parts of a territory may be prime target areas and they may receive a disproportionate amount of military attention. Underground blast-proof shelters for the government and administration discriminate against those citizens who are not regarded as key personnel. The government's notional ideas about levels of 'acceptable damage' may be unacceptable to those likely to be damaged. War casualties are discriminatory and though they may confer a benefit on others they represent a private cost of the hostilities.

Defence during hostilities concerns the probability of survival and this probability is not equal throughout the population. The position can be rationalised by the use of value judgments about the organic nature of the society in which the war is taking place—individual sacrifices can be viewed as a random cost of the privilege of living in the society being defended.

Taking these factors into consideration weakens in my view the pure public good nature of national defence once deterrence breaks down. In the nuclear age this is probably more true in view of the threatened mass and perhaps permanent destruction of society.

If defence in the deterrence phase is a pure public good for national defence how does the existence of a military alliance influence matters? In so far as the alliance strengthens deterrence—the probability of non-attack is increased—it must strengthen the public good that is provided by national defence. In an alliance each member is protected by its own efforts and the potential effort of the other members. Once the alliance is formed no member can be excluded, at least nominally, from the benefits of the alliance. No member's consumption of the benefits of the alliance is rival to any other member's consumption. An alliance appears to meet the necessary conditions of a pure public good.

There are some important qualifications to this conclusion. These, briefly, refer to the certainty of alliance response to an attack on a member. Under Article 5 of the NATO agreement an attack on one member 'shall be considered an attack against them all' (NATO 1978) and NATO members will 'assist the Party or Parties so attacked by taking forthwith, individually and in concert with other Parties, such action as it deems necessary, including the use of armed force, to restore and

maintain the security of the North Atlantic area'. To the extent
that this commitment is absolute the alliance produces a pure
public good but if any uncertainty exists about the commitment it would be prudent of individual members to maintain
some national defence forces with a capability for national
defence outside an alliance role. In these circumstances the
alliance provides a partial public good, not a pure public
good (Sandler 1977).

The economic theory of alliances is the subject of the next
chapter and these issues will be explored in greater detail.

2

Public Goods and Military Alliance

The theory of public goods is the foundation of economic theories of military alliance. In this chapter I discuss the conclusions of the small group case (Olson 1965) and how they are applied to an economic theory of alliance (Olson & Zeckhauser 1968; De Strihou 1968).

The small group case

A military alliance, such as NATO, consists of a small group of sovereign states. The behaviour of small groups in public good theory might, therefore, be of interest. Olson (1965) drew attention to the difference between a small and a large group in respect of the provision of public goods.

Individual anonymity in a large group enhances the free-rider effect and if choice is possible it is rational for the individual to avoid payment for a public good which is non-exclusive to the group members. To counter this effect the state imposes involuntary taxation on the large group to pay for public provision (Buchanan 1968).

In the small group case the situation is slightly different. Members are more visible. Differential valuation of public good provision is reflected in smaller member exploitation of larger members, where members are ranked in size by their valuation of the public good. In other words, those members of the small group who value the public good the most are exploited by those who value it less.

Olson develops his argument in the following way (with a small change in his notation): the cost of provision of a public good (as with private goods) is likely to be an increasing function of quantity—the more of the good provided the more resources that are drawn into its production. As with private goods, individuals value units of the public good differently. The value to the group of the public good will be the sum of all the individual values. The group gain, S_g, is related to the numbers in the group, the quantity of the public good and the value per unit placed on it by the members of the group. For each individual member the gain from the good being provided (S_i) is a fraction of the gain to the group (S_g) received by the individual (F_i).

The group gain is valued at V_g and the individual's gain is valued at V_i. The ratio V_i/V_g is the individual's gain F_i. The advantage for the individual of receiving the public good is the difference between V_i (his valuation of F_i) and what he contributes towards the costs of provision. This advantage is represented by A_i where $A_i = V_i - C$. The individual's advantage will change as the amount of the public good available changes because of the changes in his share of the costs:

$$\frac{dA_i}{dQ} = \frac{dV_i}{dQ} - \frac{dC}{dQ}$$

This is maximised when the addition to individual value from the public good equals the individual contribution to costs.

The optimum amount for the individual is given by:

$$\frac{dA_i}{dQ} = \frac{dV_i}{dQ} - \frac{dC}{dQ} = 0$$

$$F_i \left[\frac{dV_g}{dQ}\right] - \frac{dC}{dQ} = 0$$

$$F_i \left[\frac{dV_g}{dQ}\right] = \frac{dC}{dQ}$$

The optimal amount for the individual is reached when the rate of gain for the group times the fraction of the group gain which the individual receives equals the rate of increase in total cost of provision of the public good. For this to be so, the rate of group gain must exceed the increase in costs by the same multiple that the rate of group gain exceeds the rate of gain to the individual. It is presumed that the public good will be provided if the fraction of the group gain going to the individual exceeds the unit cost of the group gain.

$$F_i > \frac{C}{V_g}$$

Because if

$$\frac{V_i}{V_g} > \frac{C}{V_g}$$

then

$$V_i > C$$

Will the amount of the public good be optimal for the group as a whole? The optimal amount for the group will be reached when the gain to the group is increasing at the same rate as the cost of provision, i.e. when

$$\frac{dV_g}{dQ} = \frac{dC}{dQ}$$

Now each individual is motivated to demand more of the public good until

$$F_i \left[\frac{dV_g}{dQ} \right] = \frac{dC}{dQ}$$

and because the sum of all the individual fractions of the total gain must be unity ($\Sigma F_i = 1$) it follows that what the individuals will independently finance adds to the group optimum. If each individual bears a fraction of the cost of provision in proportion to his F_i it follows that the total burden will be distributed equitably according to the benefit principle, i.e. each individual pays in proportion to his individual valuation of the public good.

However, this conclusion is falsely idealistic. This is because of the public-good characteristics of non-exclusion. Each member automatically acquires the full amount of the public good that is made available to the group. The benefits available to one are available to all. If there is a member in the group with a very large F_i there is no need for other individual members to want more of the public good once this member's requirements are met. Through non-exclusion they can consume what is available from the large quantity made available by the 'largest' member.

A small group with a member who has a large F_i will bring the group closer to an optimum than a large group with small F_is. Nevertheless there will still be sub-optimal provision. The greater the disparity between the largest member of a small group and the smaller members (the more the larger member's S_i approaches S_g) the more the burden of provision of the public good will be shifted onto the larger member. The burden will not be proportionate to the benefits because of free riding by the smaller members. Without other influences this could mean the larger member carrying the entire burden of public provision.

Olson designated this behaviour as small member exploitation of the larger member. Where differential valuation is present those who value the good least (the smaller members) will exercise the option of free riding on those that value the good most (the larger members). Because of the visibility of each member's contribution in a small group free riding will take the form of disproportionate burden sharing—the largest will contribute the most. As long as the smaller members have access to the public good their bargaining position is relatively strong.

In a military alliance these conclusions are most interesting. A military alliance is a small group, it provides a public good, and there is the possibility that some members value the alliance output more than others. If the 'larger' members can be identified it should be possible to test the theory by relating valuation to contribution—the largest member(s) should contribute the largest share of the costs of mutual defence if the theory is correct. I will now turn to the economic theory of military alliance to discuss how the small-group case is applied in it and then we will look at the empirical evidence.

Economic theory of alliance

Figure 2.1 is from Olson & Zeckhauser (1968, p. 268). Defence expenditures of the country are measured on the vertical axis and valued negatively (defence expenditure is a bad: a regrettable necessity) and defence capability is measured horizontally and valued positively (ceteris paribus, capability is positively related to security). The indifference curves relating defence to non-defence goods have been cut off at the present income line and turned over. For simplicity, the cost curves are assumed to be linear (an increase in defence output leads to a proportionate increase in costs). Costs are also assumed to be identical for both the country and its partners.

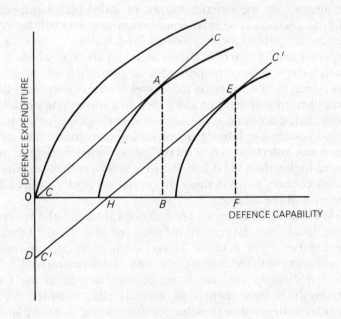

Figure 2.1

Before joining an alliance the country receives *OB* defence capability for expenditure *AB* (the point of tangency of the cost curve *OC* from the origin with the 'highest' indifference curve). Upon joining an alliance the country will benefit from the defence expenditures of its partners because defence is a public good. If the alliance expenditure on defence is represented by *OD* and a cost curve is drawn from *D* it will be tangential to an indifference curve at *E*. The country now receives *OF* defence capability. Of this capability it receives *OH* at zero cost—it is paid for by the alliance partners—and contributes *HF* itself at *EF* cost. It has more defence capability after the alliance than before (*OF* > *OB*) and at a lower cost (*EF* < *AB*). The country will be 'better off'. The income effect allows it to reduce its own defence spending and increase non-defence spending at a higher level of national security.

The amount a country spends on defence is influenced by the amount it receives in the form of a public good from the alliance and the amount the alliance spends on defence will be influenced by the defence output of individual members for similar reasons. The final equilibrium position will be determined by public good spillovers (and spillins). These can be represented by reaction curves as in Figure 2.2, which shows each party's defence spending for all possible levels of defence spending by the other. If the curves intersect there will be an equilibrium with each country spending something on defence after taking account of the other country's supply of the public good (assuming defence is not an inferior good). The curves may not intersect if one party values defence output much more highly than the other. Its curve will lie entirely outside the other country's and in these circumstances it will supply all the defence of the alliance.

Whichever country values defence capability the most will contribute the largest proportion of the costs. Olson & Zeckhauser show that the 'larger' country, defined initially as the country with the highest valuation of defence capability, will bear a disproportionate share of the burden. If the larger country's defence provision exceeds that required by the smaller country it is possible for free riding to take place. In this case the larger country could contribute up to 100 per cent

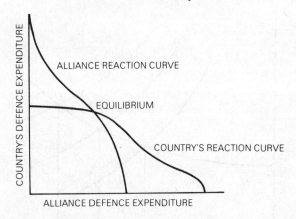

Figure 2.2

of the costs. Its share of the costs would be greater than its share of the benefits (total benefits minus the smaller country's benefits from what is provided).

There is a possible exception to this disproportionate division of the costs. This can occur when the smaller country regards defence as a superior good, i.e. when expenditure on defence increases by as much or more than income increases. In Figure 2.1 this would occur when the indifference map of the smaller member is such that any perpendicular from the ordinate intersects all indifference curves at points of equal slope. In practical terms this situation would occur when the smaller country was in severe military distress (war or invasion) and regarded alliance defence as a much-needed supplement to its own maximum contribution.

De Strihou's model

De Strihou (1968) came to conclusions similar to Olson & Zeckhauser's concerning the behaviour of members in a military alliance. His presentation was somewhat different. In Figure 2.3 there are two countries, as before, one being 'larger' than the other. In the initial position each country considers its defence needs independently of the other. Country 1 has a total

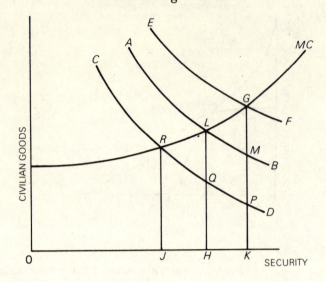

Figure 2.3

marginal rate of substitution schedule, *AB*, and country 2 has one shown as *CD*. The marginal cost curve for defence is the same for both countries and is upward sloping (suggesting that additional units of military security—however measured—cost more per unit).

Before the alliance, country 2 will provide *OJ* units of security and country 1 will provide *OH* units. If the two countries merged into one they would provide *OK* units of security through the vertical addition of their TMRS schedules (the sum of the individual marginal rate of substitution (mrs) schedules of the citizens of a country). If they form an alliance instead of merging the result will be different if military security is a public good. At *OK* each country values the marginal unit of security at less than *KG*. Country 1 values *KG* at *KM* and country 2 values *KG* at *KP*. Both countries would tend to reduce their defence expenditures.

At a combined defence output providing *OH* security country 1 will hold its defence expenditure at whatever level is needed to produce *OH* security when its own output and that of its partner's are added together. But country 2 will tend to continue to reduce its defence spending because *OH* exceeds *OJ* and as long as the alliance output is at least *OJ* its security needs are being met. The alliance output, being a public good, is available to country 2, and country 1, in order to maintain security level *OH*, will be obliged to contribute the entire cost of *OH*. Country 2 will be able to reduce its expenditures to zero which is the familiar Olson & Zeckhauser conclusion for widely divergent valuations of defence. De Strihou's model suggests that any provision of defence in excess of a smaller member's valuation (*HL* > *HQ*) will lead in the end to free riding.

De Strihou modifies that conclusion with the consideration of income effects and the partial public good nature of defence. Figure 2.4 uses transformation curves (showing the technical rate at which civilian goods can be converted into defence goods). Country 2's transformation curve for security and non-defence (civilian) goods is shown as *AB*. *CD* is its indifference curve which is tangential at *G* with the transformation curve (the marginal rate of transformation in production is equal at this point to the marginal rate of substitution in consumption).

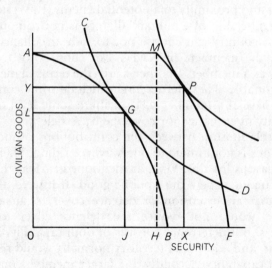

Figure 2.4

When there is no alliance, country 2 will provide *OJ* security and have *OL* resources available for civilian consumption and investment (i.e. non-defence uses). In alliance with country 1 (a 'larger' country) a new equilibrium occurs at *P*. This is brought about because *OH* security is available from country 1's defence contribution in the alliance. In effect this moves country 2's transformation curve to the right by *AM* (= *OH*). Allowing for adjustments in its shape due to increasing marginal costs of defence, the new transformation curve is tangential to a higher indifference curve at *P*. At *P* country 2 has *OX* security and *OY* civilian goods. It receives *OH* security free from country 1 and contributes *HX* security itself. This enables it to increase civilian consumption to *OY*. The alliance has produced an income effect on the country's allocation of resources between civilian and defence goods. Ceteris paribus, country 2 is better off.

There need not be an income effect as shown in Figure 2.4. The effect appears in this example because of the shape of the indifference map. It is possible for *JG* to be equal in height to *XP*, or indeed to be greater. The models do not incorporate information about levels of threat perception, geographical influences and proximity to a potential enemy. In Western countries membership of a military alliance is not compulsory and just as a country can choose not to join an alliance, such as NATO, the members of NATO can choose not to accept a country as a member. In other words the terms of membership are negotiable. These terms might include some commitment on the part of a member to contribute some level of defence capability in exchange for coverage by Article 5.

The relationship between the contributions of members of an alliance is not limited to one-way free riding. There are two main reasons for this. First, as mentioned earlier, the alliance output may not be a pure public good. If it were, this would imply that an extension of defence cover to an additional member would not reduce the defence cover to existing members. But deterrence consists of both capability and commitment, and additional territory normally would require additional capability. Secondly, the larger members may be able to negotiate terms for an extension of their own defence cover to smaller members (see Sandler 1977).

The first reason reinforces the second. The individual members are induced by the partial public good nature of the alliance output (relative uncertainty about commitment) to provide some national defence capability. The smaller members will seek to have their own survival highly valued by the larger members and will be prepared to accept conditions from the larger members to secure their undertaking to meet alliance commitments to them. Among these conditions might be a requirement that they provide national defence forces within their economic means and commit them to the alliance.

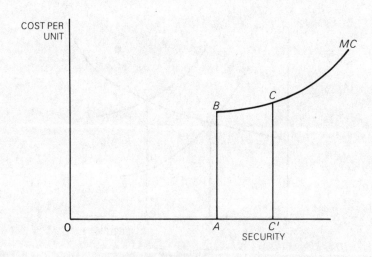

Figure 2.5

In Figure 2.5 De Strihou's representation of an alliance relationship under conditions of partial public good provision and bargaining between members is shown. *OA* is the amount of security provided automatically by the larger member at zero cost to other members. In return for this free defence the smaller member is obliged to contribute *AC'* at a marginal cost per unit rising from *AB* along the marginal cost curve *BC*.

What would happen if two countries of the same size (as defined here they both have the same valuation of defence output) formed an alliance? The situation can be illustrated as in Figure 2.6. As the countries are the same each would be represented in the pre-alliance position by TMRS CA. Each would provide ON of security at marginal cost NL.

If they form an alliance each can consume the other partner's defence provision (pure public good case). If one partner can persuade the other to provide all of the defence it provided before the alliance it could reduce its own defence outlay to zero and free ride on its partner for the same level of security as before.

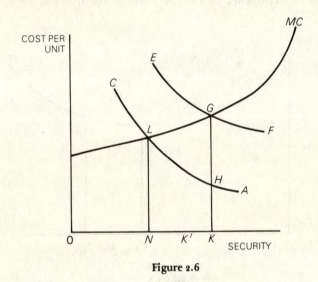

Figure 2.6

Only special circumstances would permit absolute free riding by one of the partners and therefore some other arrangement will have to be found. The combined TMRS schedules are represented by EF in Figure 2.6. The alliance security output would be OK at a marginal cost KG. Each country values OK of security at KH. If $2(KH) = KG$ there is a possible equilibrium position for the members since for more security ($OK > ON$) each member has a lower marginal cost per unit than before the alliance ($KH < NL$). If the alliance was formed to increase the amount of security available to each member, i.e. each country wants OK security but could not afford KG cost, then an allocation of costs between them in proportion to their valuation of security would be a possible solution.

Suppose that each country has joined the alliance to maintain security at ON but at a reduced cost below NL. Again they can distribute the costs on the benefit principle and each contribute half the costs so that the combined defence outlay provides ON security. In this case they have the same amount of security as before the alliance at reduced cost.

The post-alliance security output will have an upper limit of OK and a lower limit of ON. It could settle anywhere between ON and OK. The equilibrium position will depend on the perceived needs for security of the members (on our assumptions these are identical) and the willingness to share the costs equally (on our assumptions they will pay half each).

The main predictions from alliance theory are that where valuations are unequal there will be unequal shares of provision costs; in particular, that the larger members will contribute disproportionately to the common costs (Olson & Zeckhauser 1968) or, putting it another way, that the smaller members will exploit the larger members (Olson 1965; De Strihou 1968). The next chapter will look at the empirical evidence for these predictions.

3

Disproportionate Effort in Alliance

Olson & Zeckhauser (1968) derived from their model this testable hypothesis: 'In an alliance, there will be a significant positive correlation between the size of a member's national income and the percentage of its national income spent on defence.' They tested this prediction with NATO data for 1964 and found a significant and positive correlation for the ratio of defence to GNP and the size of the GNP (D/GNP to GNP). De Strihou (1968, p. 314) endorsed their conclusion: 'Given a limiting assumption, our explanations suggest, for the Western countries, a positive relationship between the share of GNP devoted to defence and the absolute amount of the GNP.' Pryor (1968, p. 98) agreed that 'the ratio of defence expenditures to the factor price GNP is statistically related (0·5 level of significance) to the absolute value of the GNP'. Hoffman (1969, p. 306) concluded that 'on the whole the figures confirm the observation that defence expenditures increase both in relative and absolute terms with economic growth'. (For a refutation of this conclusion see Kennedy 1975.) Finally, Russett (1970, p. 106) gave positive, though qualified, support to the supposed relationship between D/GNP and GNP.

This chapter will make two main points. First, the Olson & Zeckhauser model does not imply a relationship between D/GNP and GNP, except under highly restrictive assumptions. Second, the NATO data for the 1970s do not support the relationship.

The meaning of largeness

Olson & Zeckhauser are able to derive a prediction about the relationship between D/GNP and GNP by the use of two dis-

tinct meanings of largeness, one of which is simply an assertion. A 'larger' nation is 'the one that places the higher absolute value on the alliance good' (p. 269). Here largeness is
unrelated to size of the GNP because a small nation (in GNP
terms) may place a higher valuation on the alliance good than
a larger nation (in GNP terms).

The derivation of disproportionality using this concept of
largeness can be seen in an example used by Olson &
Zeckhauser (Big Atlantis and Little Atlantis) and De Strihou's
diagrammatic presentation shown in Figure 2.3.

There are two countries, Big Atlantis and Little Atlantis,
identical in every respect except that Big Atlantis has twice the
population of Little Atlantis. Per capita incomes are the same
in both countries and individual tastes are identical (the
marginal rate of substitution schedules between defence and
non-defence goods are the same for all citizens). As Big Atlantis
has twice the population of Little Atlantis it will have twice the
GNP (per capita income times population) and it will be the *larger*
country on two counts: first, the vertical summation of its
individual marginal rate of substitution (mrs) schedules will be
greater than the smaller population country which means it
values defence more, or more correctly, requires a larger
defence capability; second, it is larger than Little Atlantis in
both population and GNP. Thus, by the assumption of identical mrs schedules and a difference in population, Olson &
Zeckhauser have made inevitable the conclusions of their
model but in doing so they illegitimately use the particular circumstances of a version of their model to derive general
predictions in circumstances where it is not obvious that these
assumptions apply.

The model in Figure 2.3 is already familiar and can be
briefly summarised for recapitulation. Big Atlantis is
represented by TMRS AB and Little Atlantis by TMRS CD.
Before the alliance Big Atlantis provides itself with OH security
and Little Atlantis with OJ at a marginal cost per unit of HL
and JR respectively. In alliance the combined TMRS schedule
will be EF and defence provision will now be OK. But as
neither country values the marginal unit of security at its
marginal cost both will reduce defence expenditures—Big

Atlantis to *OH* and Little Atlantis in the end to zero.

If the alliance output is a pure public good the smaller country can free ride on the larger country. As Olson & Zeckhauser define size in two ways—valuation of the alliance output and size of GNP—they can use the conclusion of the model—small member exploitation of larger members—to predict a positive relationship between D/GNP and GNP, or, in other words, disproportionate burden sharing between members of different sizes.

If the burden were proportionate the larger member in this example would have to contribute twice the absolute amount to defence that the smaller country contributes—it being twice as big—but the same proportionate amount, i.e. their D/GNPs would be the same. But from the public good nature of the alliance output, Big Atlantis could contribute up to 100 per cent of the alliance defence instead of just twice as much as Little Atlantis. At any level of alliance contribution above twice as much as Little Atlantis, where the D/GNP ratios would be identical, Big Atlantis would be contributing a greater proportion of its GNP to defence than its partner. Its D/GNP ratio would be greater than that of Little Atlantis and the burden would therefore be shared disproportionately.

It is only if we assume identical per capita incomes and mrs schedules that the larger country is identified as the one with the larger population, and therefore the larger GNP. Remove these assumptions and GNP size will not determine which country is represented in Figure 2.3 by TMRS *AB*. To represent the larger country in this way it is necessary to create circumstances in which valuation of defence is related to the size of the GNP and graft this onto the model.

Some empirical data might help illustrate the dangers of the casual use of assumptions of this nature.

Canada is a relatively large country in GNP terms (1976 GNP was US$ 175.3 billion) and its D/GNP ratio for 1976 was 1.9 per cent. Norway is a relatively small country in GNP terms (1976 GNP was US$ 31.1 billion) and its D/GNP ratio was 3.1 per cent. Again, Israel with a US$ 12.6 billion GNP had a D/GNP ratio in 1976 of 35.3 per cent. Which country would be Big Atlantis? Certainly, TMRS schedules are not necessarily related to the absolute size of GNP. Olson & Zeckhauser's first meaning of largeness—valuation of defence output—would be more relevant in these examples than their second.

It is possible to derive a proposition that a country's D/GNP ratio will fall in an alliance compared to its pre-alliance position. In Figure 2.1 *AB*/GNP > *EF*/GNP except when defence is a superior good. But this is not the same thing as asserting that *AB*/GNP is positively related to GNP. Evidence supports the view that *AB* is positively related to the absolute size of the GNP and therefore for any given pre-alliance D/GNP the post-alliance D/GNP could be smaller but whether the larger country in GNP terms enters the alliance with a larger D/GNP than another smaller country cannot be derived from the model.

Another approach to the alleged relationship using the Olson & Zeckhauser model (Figure 2.1) could be one in which it is asserted that the larger *OD* is relative to *AB* the more the country concerned is likely to be affected by the alliance output. A large *OD* (defence contribution by the alliance) will mean that the cost curve, *C'C'*, cuts the horizontal axis further to the right. This makes *OH* relatively large. The further to the right that *C'C'* cuts the axis the closer the point of tangency of *C'C'* with an indifference curve will be to the axis. In the end it will coincide with the axis which would occur when the country receives so much of the alliance public good that it does not provide any defence for itself—it free rides.

From this approach it can be suggested that the smaller a country's defence output before the alliance (*AB*) and the larger the alliance defence output (*OD*) the more it will be affected by the alliance output (*OH*), and the more it will react by cutting its own defence provision. Conversely, the larger the country's defence output before the alliance and the smaller the alliance output the less its defence spending will fall. This could suggest that the small defence spender will cut defence more than the large defence spender on joining the alliance and if, but only if, the small defence spender has a small D/GNP ratio and the large defence spender has a larger D/GNP ratio the alliance will impose disproportionate defence burdens. But it is not necessarily the case that the D/GNP ratios are conveniently related in this way. If they are related in this way (or closely approximate to it) and the D/GNP ratios are positively related to size of GNP before the alliance it follows that as the larger country's D/GNP ratio will fall a little rather than a lot, and the small country's D/GNP ratio will fall a lot rather than a little, the large country will have a larger D/GNP after alliance than the small country. But the limitations of this argument are obvious: it is necessary to assume the conclusion of the hypothesis before it is derived from the model. Olson & Zeckhauser's model has a general validity in relating the share of defence burdens to size of the members of an alliance when by size is meant the 'absolute value of the alliance good'. But a smaller GNP member may place a higher valuation on the alliance good than a larger GNP member: in the model's general statement this smaller GNP member is the largest alliance member.

Olson & Zeckhauser extend the meaning of largeness in this way in order to test for an alleged empirical relationship which is assumed to reside in their model. In fact, their model is devoid of empirical verification in much the same way as utility theory in micro-economics. The member that values defence the most will contribute a disproportionate (i.e. larger) share of the burden simply because it values defence the most; the consumer chooses the combination of goods and services he does in order to maximise his total utility and he maximises his total utility by choosing the combination he does. There is no way of empirically testing such propositions.

If the mrs schedules of the individuals in the member countries are the same and the per capita incomes are the same, then the country with the largest population will have the largest GNP. In this case largeness by valuation and size will coincide. If the mrs schedules are the same but the per capita incomes are different then the country with the largest sum of per capita income times population will have the largest GNP but this may or may not coincide with size by valuation. If the mrs schedules are different and the per capita incomes are different and the populations are different the largest country by valuation may or may not coincide with the largest country by GNP. Once the TMRS of a member is separated from its GNP by size the prediction of a positive relationship between size of GNP and the D/GNP ratio is fragile because any level of D/GNP is now consistent with a presumption that the D/GNP ratio is related to the absolute valuation of the alliance good. The model is interesting but not verifiable; it *explains* disproportionate D/GNP ratios but not in a way that can be tested empirically. In the next section the empirical tests of the Olson & Zeckhauser hypothesis will be examined and the conclusions of this section confirmed.

Empirical evidence

Olson & Zeckhauser tested for a positive relationship between the D/GNP ratio and the absolute size of GNP for NATO members in the years 1960 and 1964. They found significant positive correlation coefficients (Spearman Rank) of 0·635 and 0·490 respectively. Iceland was excluded from the calculations on the grounds that it did not have defence expenditures though its inclusion would of course have strengthened the relationship expressed in the values of the coefficients.

De Strihou (1968, p. 317) ran a similar test using the logarithm of the NATO members' GNP in US dollars for the years 1955 and 1963. He found a positive r^2 in 1955 of 0·66 for 15 NATO members and 0·83 for 14 NATO members in 1963. In the latter year he excluded Portugal from the list because of its relatively high defence expenditures arising from its colonial wars in Africa. He also found a higher r^2 of 0·89 when some low GNP members with high D/GNP ratios (Greece, Portugal and Turkey) were excluded and four small GNP and neutralist countries (Sweden, Finland, Austria and Ireland) included.

Pryor (1968, p. 97) tested the relationship for the years 1956 and 1962. He included a variable for per capita incomes and found r^2 values of 0·50 and 0·49 respectively. Russett (1970, p. 104) tested for the relationship using a Kendal Tau statistic and he found similar but slightly lower coefficients for the years 1950 and 1967. He concluded that 'the general pattern holds and the exceptions fit within the broader context of the theory'.

In Table 3.1 the D/GNP ratios for 14 NATO members have

Table 3.1 Correlation coefficients of D/GNP with absolute GNP for 14
NATO members, 1960–75

Year	Spearman Rank	Kendal Tau
1960	0·60	0·42
1962	0·50	0·40
1966	0·42	0·32
1967	0·41	0·24
1968	0·30	0·20
1969	0·27	0·14
1970	0·19	0·10
1971	0·14	0·11
1972	0·18	0·11
1973	0·18	0·12
1974	0·25	0·12
1975	0·30	0·09

Sources: calculated from data in World Bank (1977); IISS, (1974, 1978);
NATO (1976)

been correlated with the absolute size of their GNPs using the
Spearman Rank Order Correlation Coefficient and the Kendal
Tau statistic. The coverage is for years between 1960 and 1975.
The high and positive correlations found by the authors
quoted above are confirmed in the Spearman test up to 1967
but then they fall away. Likewise with the Kendal Tau statistic.
It would appear that the postulated relationship suggested by
the model weakened by the end of the 1960s and was no longer
operating in the 1970s.

Such explanations as there are of individual NATO
members' behaviour in respect of their D/GNP ratios invite the
conclusion that the use of the model to explain that behaviour
through the supposed relationship is superfluous. If we can
explain behaviour as an exception why use a model to set a
standard which every member appears to depart from?

Individual adjustments can be made to the sample to improve its statistical correlation. De Strihou, for example,
eliminates Greece, Portugal and Turkey, in four of his eight
tests for a relationship. In three others he adds some small
non-members of NATO to the sample. Both these adjustments

improve the value of the coefficient as would be expected when small GNP countries with large D/GNPs are substituted by small GNP countries with small D/GNPs. The argument in favour of this adjustment is the alleged spillover of an alliance output onto neighbours who are not members—they benefit from the alliance by their geographical proximity to the contested territory of the alliances in confrontation. The argument against such an adjustment, particularly when substitutions take place, is that the implication is that small non-members exploit the alliance more than small members and, further, medium-sized members exploit the alliance more than small members. This last follows from the fact of substitution which would not be necessary if the small members' D/GNPs were not so inconveniently out of line with the prediction.

Portugal was engaged in African wars during the 1960s and this had a side effect in raising the D/GNP ratio. It is possible to argue that this additional military effort fell outside the alliance objectives and therefore ought not to be included in a test for free riding in an alliance. When Portugal is excluded the Spearman coefficient remains significant up to 1974. Since the end of African hostilities Portugal's defence expenditure has been reduced and the D/GNP ratio has been falling. But the elimination of Greece and Turkey is less plausible in this kind of test. True, they have been building up defence forces as a result of their mutual hostility but they have also had relatively high D/GNPs throughout the history of NATO. Their defence expenditures can be reduced by counting military aid as part of alliance output.

The D/GNP ratio measures the budgetary cost of defence, not the resource cost. Members with conscript armies are able to reduce the budgetary cost by the difference in conscript wages and civilian market wages, net of an allowance for the additional manpower required in a conscript force for training purposes (Hackel 1970, pp. 18–22). In the case of France and Germany this could add a percentage point to their D/GNP ratios and may be important in the cases of other members with conscript forces (Norway, Netherlands, Belgium, Denmark, Italy, Greece, Turkey, Portugal and, until recently, America).

How satisfactory such adjustments are is a matter of judgment. Germany's relatively low D/GNP could perhaps be explained by alliance sensitivity to 'excessive' German military power; Britain's relatively high D/GNP could be explained by a view of the British administration's failure, if not refusal, to recognise its less than great power status; France's relatively high D/GNP could be explained by its political position of distrust of American intentions towards the defence of Europe and Canada's low D/GNP by its geographical position and so on.

Defence and GNP

Olson & Zeckhauser provided no evidence for their assertion that a large country (by GNP) would value defence more than a small country. It is hard to justify this view except in the Russian and American cases but even in these the relationship is reversed between them—Russia the smaller of the two by GNP has the largest of the two D/GNPs (Cockle 1978).

In the world as a whole D/GNP is not related to size of GNP. Quite the reverse in many cases. In Table 3.2 the D/GNP ratios for a large number of countries are shown rank ordered by size. What is immediately apparent is the number of low GNP countries that have relatively high D/GNP rankings (Kennedy 1975).

The time series data for NATO members also show a steady downward trend in D/GNP ratios. Whatever the connection between D/GNP and GNP it cannot be argued that absolute size of the GNP pushes up the D/GNP ratio—all the economies in Table 3.3 were growing during the time period yet their D/GNPs were tending to fall in the main. The share of defence in state budgets was also falling (Table 3.4).

It is only when we turn to the correlation between absolute defence expenditures and size of GNP that we find a highly significant and positive relationship (Table 3.5). The Spearman Rank coefficient reaches values in the high 0·9s. This relationship is to be expected. The larger a country's GNP the greater the amount that is spent on defence. For the majority of countries in NATO the D/GNP ratio is declining though

Table 3.2 Defence expenditures as a percentage of GNP (D/GNP) in selected countries, rank ordered, 1967–76

Country	1967	1969	1971	1974	1976	
Israel	11·5	24·1	23·9	31·8	35·3	
Egypt	12·7	13·0	21·7	22·8	37·0	
						——— 20%
Jordan	11·1	21·0	11·3	12·1	11·7	
Syria	10·7	11·6	9·8	11·0	15·1 (1975)	
Iran	4·9	5·0	8·5	14·0	12·0	
						——— 10%
Taiwan	7·9	9·2	9·8	7·2	na	
America	9·5	8·7	7·3	6·1	6·0	
Iraq	9·1	9·6	6·5	18·7	na	
Portugal	7·2	6·7	6·3	6·6	3·9	
Germany (E)	3·7	5·9	5·9	5·4	6·0	
Singapore	2·2	4·9	6·3	5·1	na	
Czechoslovakia	5·7	5·6	5·8	3·8	3·5	
Korea (S)	3·9	4·0	5·1	4·3	5·1 (1975)	
Yugoslavia	5·2	5·6	4·7	5·1	5·6 (1975)	
Britain	5·7	5·0	4·7	5·1	5·1	
Pakistan	3·6	3·4	4·2	8·4	6·2	
Turkey	4·4	4·2	3·3	3·7	5·6	
Greece	4·4	5·1	3·3	4·0	5·5	
						——— 5%
Malaysia	4·1	3·6	4·3	3·8	4·0 (1975)	
Thailand	2·5	3·7	3·9	3·2	3·7 (1975)	
Sweden	3·9	3·9	3·7	3·4	3·7	
Hungary	2·6	3·4	3·5	2·4	2·6	
India	3·3	3·5	3·4	2·7	3·0 (1975)	
Italy	3·1	2·7	2·6	2·9	2·6	
						——— 2%

Source: IISS (1972, 1978), extracted and re-arranged

their GNPs are growing, which implies an income elasticity for defence that is positive but less than one (its Engels curve is concave from below). This is true for defence as a whole but it may be that for particular types of defence capability the income elasticity of demand may be positive and greater than one (the Engels curve for these items is convex from below). This might explain why the absolute amount of expenditure on defence was substantially higher for the richer countries in the world than for the poorer countries—they do not just buy

Table 3.3 Defence expenditures as a percentage of GNP for NATO members, 1967–76

Country	1967	1968	1969	1970	1971	1972	1973	1974	1975	1976
America	9·5	9·3	8·4	7·7	6·7	6·1	6·1	6·1	5·9	6·0
Germany	4·7	3·6*	4·0	3·4	4·1	4·1	4·1	4·3	4·4	4·2
France	5·0	4·8	3·5	3·5	3·7	3·5	3·5	3·6	3·9	3·7
Britain	5·7	5·4	5·0	4·8	5·2	4·9	4·9	5·1	4·9	5·1
Italy	3·1	3·0	2·9	2·7	3·1	3·0	3·0	2·9	2·6	2·6
Canada	2·8	2·7	2·4	2·1	2·2	2·0	2·0	2·1	2·2	1·9
Belgium	2·9	2·9	2·8	2·6	2·8	2·7	2·7	2·8	3·0	3·0,
Netherlands	3·8	3·6	3·8	3·5	3·4	3·3	3·3	3·4	3·6	3·4
Denmark	2·7	2·8	2·5	2·5	2·4	2·1	2·1	2·2	2·2	2·8
Turkey	4·4	4·5	3·6	3·5	4·2	4·1	4·1	3·7	9·0	5·6
Norway	3·5	3·7	3·8	3·5	3·3	3·2	3·2	3·1	3·1	3·1
Greece	4·4	4·9	4·9	3·5	4·6	4·1	4·1	4·0	6·9	5·5
Portugal	7·2	7·4	5·9	6·1	6·9	6·2	6·2	6·6	6·0	3·9
Luxembourg	1·2	1·0	0·9	0·9	0·9	0·8	0·8	0·9	1·1	1·2

Source: IISS (1971, 1978)
* excludes contribution to Berlin forces
Note: D/GNP ratios vary according to source and these might not correspond to ratios published officially in member countries

Table 3.4 Defence expenditure as a percentage of state budgets for NATO members, 1974–7

Country	1974	1975	1976	1977
Belgium	9·8	10·0	10·2	10·4
Britain	12·9	11·6	11·0	11·4
Canada	14·3	11·9	10·9	na
Denmark	7·4	7·3	7·4	6·8
France	20·3	20·2	20·6	20·4
Germany*	28·8	29·2	28·9	29·2
Greece	25·2	25·5	26·0	na
Italy	11·0	9·7	8·6	8·3
Luxembourg	3·5	3·0	2·9	2·9
Netherlands	12·2	11·0	9·8	9·7
Norway	8·5	8·2	7·6	9·9
Portugal	47·3	35·2	na	19·2
Turkey	19·2	26·6	29·4	21·1
USA	26·5	23·8	26·0	24·4

Source: IISS (1978)
* includes contribution to Berlin forces
Note: differences in composition of state budgets make inter-country comparisons meaningless

Table 3.5 Correlation between amount spent on defence and absolute GNP
for NATO members, 1970–6 (Spearman Rank)

Year	Coefficient
1970	0·94
1971	0·97
1972	0·96
1973	0·97
1974	0·96
1975	0·96
1976	0·97

Source: calculated from data in IISS (1971 ... 1978)

more defence capability, they buy different capabilities. The
absolute amounts spent on defence in NATO in US dollars for
1970–6 are shown in Table 3.6.

The greater the absolute size of a country's GNP the greater
the absolute amount a given D/GNP ratio will make available.
Thus, for a relatively smaller D/GNP ratio a larger country can
provide a larger amount of defence capability. It is defence

Table 3.6 Total defence expenditures of NATO members in US $ million,
1970–6

Country	1970	1971	1972	1973	1974	1975	1976
America	76 507	78 743	83 400	79 500	85 906	88 903	102 191
Germany*	7 067	6 860	9 531	14 044	16 688	19 540	18 758
France	5 982	5 202	6 238	8 438	9 970	13 984	12 857
Britain	5 950	6 108	6 968	8 673	10 410	11 118	10 734
Italy	2 599	2 651	3 251	3 997	4 142	4 700	3 821
Canada	1 931	1 688	1 966	2 154	2 965	2 965	3 231
Belgium	688	594	723	990	1 506	1 971	2 013
Netherlands	1 106	1 166	1 568	2 102	2 406	2 978	2 825
Denmark	368	410	441	568	741	939	861
Turkey	503	446	568	803	1 173	2 200	2 800
Norway	376	411	462	666	723	929	909
Greece	453	338	495	552	1 807	1 435	2 276
Portugal	398	398	425	523	1 000	1 088	748
Luxembourg	8	9	10	17	19	22	23

Source: IISS (1971, 1978), extracted and re-arranged
* includes contributions to Berlin forces

capability that is the objective of defence spending, not the D/GNP ratio. Indeed, the most pressure for reducing the amount spent on defence comes from within the high GNP countries, as alternative expenditure programmes compete for the resources that are available.

The amount a country spends on defence is related to a non-economic category, threat perception. It would appear that attempts to measure threat perception are bound to fail because ultimately threat perception is reflected in the size of the defence budget. 'How much is enough?' is a subjective question. Trying to give an empirical content to a tautological relationship has little scientific meaning. Olson & Zeckhauser's model is a useful step in understanding alliance economics but their empirical prediction leads to a spurious result.

4

Burden-sharing Criteria

The economic theory of alliance suggests that the largest member, i.e. the one that values the alliance output the most, will bear a disproportionate share of the burden of provision. This raises normative questions of equity and fairness. Olson & Zeckhauser note however that 'no moral conclusions can follow solely from any purely logical model' (1968, p. 278). Indeed, they point out that disproportionate burden sharing rests on the national interests of the members: it is in the interests of the large member to supply the bulk of the defence output of the alliance and it is in the interests of the smaller members to free ride. The result of pursuing national interests in the alliance is sub-optimal provision of the alliance output (in Figure 2.3 the combined TMRS schedules *EF* require a defence outlay of *OK* but the equilibrium outlay is less than this if members act in their national interests). Because the outlay is sub-optimal it might be possible to make a change in the way the alliance output is provided that moves the output towards the optimum and thereby leaves every member better off. In this way the normative issues of equity and fairness can be given a positive purpose.

By sub-optimal the theory appears to mean that alliance will provide less defence than would be the case if each country acted on its own. By analogy, this suggests that optimal provision of police services would be achieved if each citizen provided his own, and anything less than this is sub-optimal. In this case the optimum would be grossly inefficient.

In this chapter I will discuss the contributions of economic theory to equity issues in the burden-sharing context. Once again the discussion is necessarily a summary one.

The benefit approach

Smith (1776) characteristically set a criterion for public provision that appears to be a combination of the benefit and ability-to-pay approaches: 'The expense of defending the society, and that of supporting the dignity of the chief magistrate, are both laid out for the general benefit of the whole society. It is reasonable, therefore, that they should be defrayed by the general contribution of the whole society; all the different members contributing, as nearly as possible, in proportion to their respective abilities.' (Smith 1776, book V, ch. 1.) But where the beneficiaries of public activity could be identified, as Smith believed they could be in education, justice, travel on public highways and certain public works, it was necessary to charge some or all of the costs in proportion to the identified benefit. He believed it was 'unjust that the whole society should contribute towards an expense, of which the benefit is confined to a part of society'.

Following Smith a discussion has continued on the merits of using the benefit approach to allocate costs of common activities among the persons affected by the activity in proportion to their benefits. John Stuart Mill summarised the benefit approach (which he went on to criticise) in his *Principles of Political Economy* (1848):

> What pleases them is to regard the taxes paid by each member of the community as an equivalent for value received, in the shape of service to himself; and they prefer to rest the justice of making each contribute in proportion to his means, upon the ground, that he who has twice as much property to be protected, receives, on an accurate calculation, twice as much protection, and ought, on the principles of bargain and sale, to pay twice as much for it.

In the context of the Olson & Zeckhauser model this could be taken as a statement in favour of proportionality—Big Atlantis should pay twice as much as Little Atlantis.

However, Mill was stating the benefit case in order to criticise it. He went on to state that if the beneficiaries of protection were to pay in proportion to their benefits, there would be a manifestly unjust result which is the 'reverse of the true idea of distributive justice, which consists not in imitating but in redressing the inequalities and wrongs of nature' (book V, ch. 2).

The idea of the benefit approach had a resurgence in the marginalist revolution in economic theory towards the end of the nineteenth century. Italian economists contributed much to this resurgence. (Translations of writings from Pantaleoni, Mazzola and Viti de Marco, among others, can be found in Musgrave & Peacock 1958.) Mazzola, for instance, attempted to take account of the non-exclusion characteristic of public goods in a proposal for a pricing policy based on the utilities of the public good to the individual. Payment must be made according to the marginal evaluation of the utility from the good: 'The formation of the prices of public goods comes about in such wise that in any economic unit the degrees of final utility of public goods are, after the distribution of public burdens, equal' (Musgrave & Peacock 1958, p. 46). As payment involves a disutility from sacrifice of alternatives the net effect of the utility of the public good minus the disutility of payment would equalise utility among the individuals receiving the public good.

Knut Wicksell developed the benefit approach by integrating it with a theory of political democracy. He endorsed the benefit principle of *Leistung und Gegenleistung* (a reciprocal relationship between the individual and state in which the individual enjoys a benefit from what the state provides and pays for the cost according to the benefit). Wicksell wrote:

> With all its clumsiness the theory of *Leistung und Gegenleistung* had at least the virtue of maintaining some sort of contact with the other, the expenditure, side of the public economy. That theory provided something like an upper limit to the concrete amount of taxes by rejecting any public expenditure, along with its companion tax levy, which failed to render each taxpayer a service corresponding to this payment. Justice would thereby have been done at least to the extent that each man received his money's worth. (Musgrave & Peacock 1958, p. 75)

How did he propose to apply the benefit principle? No one

person, be he ever so clever, can decide the issue of the community's gain in utility against its loss in private expenditure. Only the individual knows whether the benefits equal, or otherwise, his sacrifice of private means to meet the costs. A community of individuals in a democracy can decide the issue by voting:

> ... when individuals or groups find or believe they find that for them the marginal utility of a given public service does not equal the marginal utility of the private goods they have to contribute, then these individuals or groups will, without fail, feel overburdened. It will be no consolation to them to be assured that the utility of public services as a whole far exceeds the total value of the individual sacrifices. (Ibid p. 79)

Such individuals or groups can avoid a burden of this kind by voting simultaneously against the proposed expenditure and the means by which it is to be paid in the form of taxes. Wicksell went on to his famous unanimity rule for public decisions which would ensure that there was no burden among payers (he ignored the possibility of a disutility among non-receivers). But he went on to qualify unanimity with simple majority voting on certain issues, qualified majority voting and proportional voting on other issues.

Voluntary exchange

Economic theorists continued with efforts to integrate benefit theory into the theory of private markets. Foremost among these attempts was that of the Swedish economist, Erik Lindhal (1919). I will examine his contribution and that of Bowen (1948) in this section.

Lindhal linked the determination of the amount of public expenditure with the distribution of the burden—who paid what share of the total cost?—and sought to derive a mechanism that was akin to that of the market for private goods. I will outline Lindhal's theory of voluntary exchange, following Johansen (1965).

Assume two social groups in a community with pre-tax incomes R_a and R_b respectively such that total community income

$R = R_a + R_b$. The burden of public expenditure is divided between the two groups such that $G = h + (1 - h)$, where G is government expenditure, h is the share of G paid for by A and $(1 - h)$ is the share of G paid for by B. If the private expenditure of A is X and the private expenditure of B is Y, then

$$X + hG = R_a \quad \text{and} \quad Y + (1 - h)G = R_b$$

It follows that $X + Y + G = R$. The utility that A gets from private and public expenditure is some function of those expenditures and likewise in the case of B:

$$U_a = F_a(X,G) \quad \text{and} \quad U_b = F_b(Y,G)$$

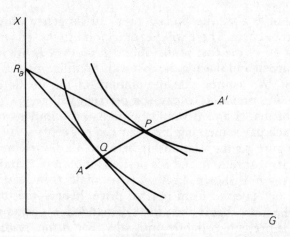

Figure 4.1

A's preferences for private and public expenditures can be represented as in Figure 4.1. A's utility (F_a) is represented by a set of indifference curves and his budget constraint by the usual budget line corresponding to $X + hG = R_a$. In Figure 4.1 two budget lines are shown tangential to indifference curves at Q and P. The slope of the budget line represents different values of h (A's share of government expenditure) and the steepest budget line corresponds to the higher value of h (the greater h, the smaller X). AA' is the locus of points where the changing

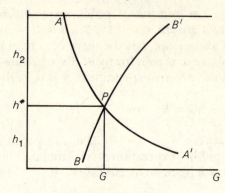

Figure 4.2

values of h alter the budget point of tangency with an in-difference curve. There will be some point to the left where A is paying all of the cost of the public good ($h = 1$). By reducing this burden and sharing the cost with B, utility for A can be in-creased. We assume that the amount of the public good of which A is prepared to pay 100 per cent will be less than the amount that A and B would be prepared jointly to supply if they each pay something less than 100 per cent.

In Figure 4.2 the relationship between A's desired amount of G and its cost ratio h, and B's desired amount of G and its cost ratio $(1 - h)$ is shown. In A's case as h falls G increases which would be expected from normal price theory—the lower the price the more that is likely to be demanded. B's demand curve for G is presented slightly unusually. For B the 'price' of the public good is the reverse of that for A—the smaller h becomes the larger $(1 - h)$ must become. Thus, if h falls, which induces A to prefer more of G, $(1 - h)$ must rise, which will induce B to prefer less of G. B's demand curve is shown rising from left to right instead of falling from left to right.

The interactions between A and B for alternative burdens can be seen in the figure. If h is given a value, say h_1, this would prompt A to opt for a large G but B is unlikely to agree to this as a low h means a high $(1 - h)$. B would prefer a low G for this distribution of the burden. Conversely, if h was to have a high value, say h_2, A would want a small G while B at that distribution would want a high G. Either of these distributions of the cost would be unpopular with one of the members of the community.

From Figure 4.2 there is one share arrangement $(h = \overset{*}{h})$ which they can both agree upon and which divides the cost such that $h + (1 - h) = 1$. The exact ratio of $h/(1 - h)$ will depend on the relative preferences for G in the two groups and also on the relative bargaining power if the two groups are unequal in economic circumstances. The implication of the model is that each group will make offers for cost sharing that moves them towards $\overset{*}{h}$. If, for instance, the price of G for A was high $(h = h_2)$ it would pay B to offer to pay more of the cost, i.e. to increase $(1 - h)$, to get more G provided. Each group would volunteer to take on a larger share of the burden if the alternative was too small a provision of G because the other party regarded the proposed cost sharing inequitable. The burden shares are zero sum (what one gains the other loses) but the benefits of the public good, through non-exclusion, are non-zero sum—they can both be made better off by an arrangement that increases the amount of G provided. Lindhal believed that the voluntary exchange process was akin to that of a private market.

Bowen's model

Howard Bowen (1948) put forward a simplification of the voluntary exchange model which states the benefit approach in the clearest manner. In Figure 4.3 two tax payers, a and b, have to decide on the amount of a public good to be provided and the share of the costs. The two tax payers have different preferences for the public good, shown by two different demand schedules. Because it is a pure public good the combined demand curve for the good is the vertical sum of the individual demands, $a + b$. The public good is produced under conditions of increasing marginal costs, MC.

The intersection of the MC curve with the demand curve for the public good, $a + b$, determines the quantity of the public good required by the community, OP, which simultaneously determines the quantity of the private good available to the in-

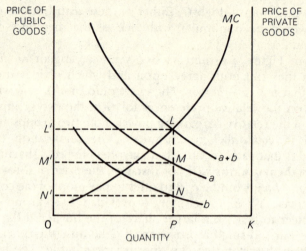

Figure 4.3

dividuals, *KP*. The quantity *OP* of the public good costs *PL* per unit, or in total, *OP* × *PL*. Each individual contributes his marginal valuation of the public good times the amount of the good available (under non-exclusion the same amount is available to both individuals). Thus, *b* pays *PN* per unit (in total, *PN* × *OP*) and *a* pays *PM* per unit (in total, *PM* × *OP*). *PN* + *PM* = *PL* and the cost of the public good (*OP* × *PL*) is met by the sum of each individual's share (*OP* [*PN* + *PM*] = *OP* × *PL*).

In Figure 4.4 Bowen's model is applied to a military alliance. Security is measured on the horizontal axis and the costs of defence on the vertical axis. In this model there are three members of the alliance, *X*, *Y* and *Z*. Member *X* values the benefits received from the alliance by the marginal benefit schedule MB_x, member *Y* by MB_y and member *Z* by MB_z. The downward slope of these schedules arises from the assumption that the more units of something that are available the less each incremental unit is valued.

The marginal benefit of security for the alliance in total is the vertical sum of the individual marginal benefit schedules, MB_{x+y+z}. The alliance provides *OP* security (where

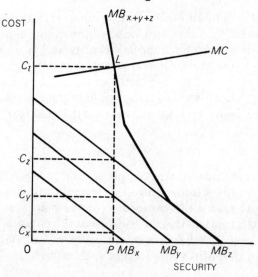

Figure 4.4

MB_{x+y+z} intersects the marginal cost schedule, MC). The cost of OP security to the alliance is OC_t and this cost is shared out among the members according to their valuation of the benefits of OP security. Member X contributes OC_x, member Y contributes OC_y and member Z contributes OC_z. These contributions sum to OC_t.

The elegance of benefit models such as Bowen's is attractive to some economists and policy makers but the problem of free riding is only assumed away—it remains the practical obstacle to their implementation. In Figure 4.4 any combination of security provision by Y and Z will provide the security level desired by X because their marginal valuations of the benefits of security lie outside the MB_x of X. By failing to reveal true preferences X can free ride on the other members of the alliance.

Other problems abound, even if revealed preference is honest. There is a severe information problem. Members have to have perfect information about the level of security successive levels of expenditure on defence will bring. In the individual version of Bowen's model this is critical. Citizens are in legal jeopardy if they seek detailed information of their own country's provision for national security and face prosecution under such laws as the Official Secrets Act. Attempts have been made to get round the problems of revealed preference most notably by Samuelson (1954, 1955), Musgrave (1966, 1969) but see also McGuire and Aaron (1969) and Buchanan (1968).

Ability to pay

Smith's (1776) maxim that people should pay for the benefits they receive 'in proportion to the revenue which they respectively enjoy under the protection of the state' has been put forward as a burden-sharing formula at the national and international level. The best statement in favour of the ability-to-pay approach is Mill's (1848, book V, ch. 2):

> As a government ought to make no distinction of persons or classes in the strength of their claims on it, whatever sacrifices it requires from them should be made to bear as nearly as possible with the same pressure upon all, which, it must be observed, is the mode by which least sacrifice is occasioned by the whole. If any one bears less than his fair share of the burden, some other person must suffer more than his share, and the alleviation to the one is not, *caeteris paribus*, so great a good to him, as the increased pressure upon the other is an evil. Equality of taxation therefore, as a maxim of politics, means equality of sacrifice. It means apportioning the contribution of each person towards the expenses of government, so that he shall feel neither more nor less inconvenienced from his share of the payment than every other person experiences from his. This standard, like other standards of perfection, cannot be completely realised; but the first object in every practical discussion should be, to know what perfection is.

Mill went on to state a burden-sharing maxim:

> ... in a case of voluntary subscription for a purpose in which all are interested, all are thought to have done their part fairly when each has contributed according to his means, that is, has made an equal sacrifice for the common object ... (Ibid.)

Can these principles be applied? There are two elements to an answer. First, what is meant by *means* and second, what is meant by *equality of sacrifice*?

An individual's means appear to have been settled by practical experience of taxation policy. Taxes fall on many economic transactions and on stocks of wealth. At the national level international comparability of statistical representation of the GNP and its related per capita income statistic suggests that a measure, however qualified, of a nation's means is available.

Measuring the equality of sacrifice is a more elusive task, which has prompted an interesting and elegant discussion for several decades (Edgeworth 1897 (1925); Musgrave 1959; Allan 1971). The discussion can be summarised by reference to Figure 4.5.

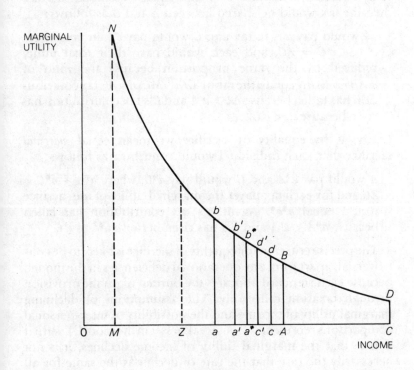

Figure 4.5

Two individuals, *A* and *C,* are represented in the figure. Individual *A* has an income including subsistence (*OM*) of *OA* and individual *C* has an income including subsistence of *OC*. The government needs to levy a tax of *ZC* to meet its expenditure programme. What concepts of equality of sacrifice can be illustrated using the figure that would raise this amount?

If by equality of sacrifice we mean equal *absolute* sacrifice then the tax would be shared by *A* and *C* as follows:

A would pay *aA* tax and *C* would pay *cC* tax, where $aA + cC = ZC$ and each would have their total utility reduced by the same amount because the area under the marginal utility of income schedule *NQ* for each individual has been reduced by the same absolute amount such that $aABb = cCDd$.

If by equality of sacrifice we mean equal *proportional* sacrifice then the tax would be shared between *A* and *C* as follows:

A would pay *a'A* in tax and *C* would pay *c'C* in tax, where $a'A + c'C = ZC$, and each would have their total utility reduced by the same proportion because the ratio of $a'ABb'/MABN$ equals the ratio $c'CDd'/MCDN$. *A*'s tax contribution has fallen because $aA > a'A$ and *C*'s tax contribution has risen because $cC < c'C$.

Lastly, if by equality of sacrifice we mean equal *marginal* sacrifice then each individual would contribute as follows:

A would pay *a*A* and *C* would pay *a*C*, where $a*A + a*C = ZC$ and for each tax payer the marginal utility of the sacrifice would equal $a*b*$. Again *A*'s tax contribution has fallen because $a*A < a'A$ and *C*'s has risen because $a*C > c'C$.

The precise criterion for equality of sacrifice is likely to be controversial, apart from any operational deficiencies in the model, because each standard allocates the burden of public provision through taxation differently. The assumptions of declining marginal utility of income and the possibility of inter-personal comparisons represent serious weaknesses in the model. Even if it is true that the marginal utility of income declines, it is not necessarily the case that the rate of decline is the same for all individuals.

Equi-marginal sacrifice pushed to the limit implies equality of post-tax incomes (*Oa** in Figure 4.5) among tax payers and if the revenue required is extremely large it could imply equality of all incomes.

In the case of an international alliance the operational value of a proposal that post-tax incomes of the members will be equalised is not likely to be very great. Where the GNPs (incomes) of the members are widely divergent, as they are in NATO, the burden of defence provision would be placed on the higher income member(s) and indeed could be carried entirely by them if the total defence outlay required by the alliance was met before their GNPs were reduced sufficiently to bring them into equality with the smaller GNP countries.

Progressivity

If the attempt to found an ability-to-pay approach to taxation on the questionable assumptions of declining marginal utility of income and inter-personal comparisons is unconvincing it nevertheless has to be faced that countries operate taxation policies for their national purposes *as if* diminishing marginal utility of income is present and *as if* comparisons between individuals are possible. There has always been some relationship between taxation—at least in principle—and means. Governments, to a greater or lesser extent, impose some proportion of their tax revenue positively with ability to pay through progressivity schedules. Society seems to take the view that the marginal utility of income declines (the more income one has the less a marginal unit is valued—a pound to a poor man is worth more than a pound to a millionaire), or it ought to be treated as if it does.

That the rich should pay more is a well established value judgment but how much more is a matter of deep, controversial and prolonged discussion. There are several rates of progression in operation in the world, as it is impossible to arrive at a standard progressivity schedule when judgment, not economics, plays the major role. If some form of progressivity is to be applied to alliance contributions we cannot go far wrong if we apply the progressivity rates that individual countries apply to their own citizens on the grounds that, presumably, what is equitable and fair for their own people is equitable and fair for themselves in their international relations.

Under a proportional tax system all taxpayers contribute the same proportion of their income in taxation; under a progressive tax system the larger a taxpayer's income the more the tax contribution that must be paid—it is disproportionate in fact. Which is the fairest system, proportional or disproportional, is a normative question though from observation there is a preference, in an equity sense, for progressive rates at least within the limits of established progressivity rates used by countries. If a particular rate lies beyond the upper limits of progressivity it is possible to claim an unfair burden as Pincus does in respect of the contribution of America to NATO defence which he claimed (1965, p. 76) was 'paying more than its share of combined NATO defense expenditures, according to all but the most progressive exchange rate formulas, and to any real income formula'.

In general we can state the conditions for progressivity and proportionality as follows:

y = income, t = amount of tax and the amount of tax is a function of income:

$$t = t(y)$$

disposable income will be:

$$y - t(y)$$

the effective tax rate is:

$$\bar{t}(y) = \frac{t(y)}{y}$$

the marginal tax rate will be:

$$t'(y) = \frac{dt(y)}{dy}$$

and a tax will be progressive when:

$$t'(y) > \bar{t}(y)$$

it will be proportional when:

$$t'(y) = \bar{t}(y)$$

and a tax will be regressive when:

$$t'(y) < \bar{t}(y)$$

These considerations provide an insight into the burden-sharing debate in an alliance. The disproportion predicted by Olson & Zeckhauser's model, which arises from the public good provided by the alliance, may indeed be an objective of a burden-sharing agreement based on a progressive ability-to-pay approach. In other words breaking with burden sharing according to benefit and moving towards burden sharing according to ability to pay might involve structured disproportion in the alliance, with the largest, in GNP terms, contributing the most, absolutely and proportionally, to the common costs.

Comparability

I will conclude this chapter with a brief discussion of comparability of means at the international level. NATO members vary in their GNPs and per capita incomes. The level of per capita income between members varies and so does the distribution of incomes within member states. How can we make comparisons?

One solution is to convert national figures into a common currency (usually the American dollar) using official exchange rates. But official exchange rates may not reflect the true relative position and, with fluctuations on the scale experienced in the 1970s, it may be arbitrary to use one rate rather than another. A suggested alternative system of comparison is the purchasing power parity method (Kravis *et al.* 1975). This attempts to derive an exchange rate between two currencies that reflects the ratio of price indices in the countries or the change in relative prices. This brings into the calculations the sometimes substantial number of non-traded goods and services and the rate of inflation:

$$R_{ab} = \frac{\text{Foreign price index}}{\text{Home price index}}$$

or

$$\frac{R_{ab}1}{R_{ab}0} = \frac{\dfrac{P_a1}{P_a0}}{\dfrac{P_b1}{P_b0}}$$

where R_{ab} is the price of foreign currency in terms of home currency (David 1972).

Countries with similar GNPs or similar per capita GNPs might still not be strictly comparable even assuming a meaningful exchange rate for their currencies could be devised. If one of the countries had a sustained and substantial deficit on its balance of payments and the other a sustained and substantial surplus would they still have the same ability to pay? To what extent should the local benefits of military expenditure by the deficit country in the surplus country be taken into account? These issues will surface again in a later chapter. The broad principle of equity and fairness may be endorsed by all members, but the problem is to find a formula that meets what everybody's ideas (and interests) lead them to support.

5

Application of the Criteria to NATO

The widely held, and applied, value judgment that individuals should contribute towards public expenditure in proportion to their abilities to pay forms the basis of the criteria for burden sharing in an alliance which will be examined in this chapter. The widespread use of ability-to-pay criteria does not in itself confirm their philosophical assumptions and to some extent this is reflected in the varying degrees of their use in member states, as seen in the different shares of taxation raised by direct or indirect means.

Equity as a maxim

Equal treatment of equals is the root of the ability-to-pay approach. Persons with equal incomes *and* circumstances are to be treated equally for taxation purposes. It follows that persons with unequal incomes or circumstances are to be treated unequally. How to define income and circumstance is the major practical test of the principle of equality of treatment and the existence of considerable tax law, not to mention the considerable business of tax advice and avoidance, testifies to the complexities involved in translating even a widely held principle into practical proposals. These problems might be thought to increase when the possible application of the principle is proposed for the international arena.

Equal treatment of equals (horizontal equity) and unequal treatment of unequals (vertical equity) are logical applications of the principles of ability to pay and equity (Musgrave 1959) but how can they be applied to burden sharing in NATO?

First, agreement must be reached on how each member's share of the burden is to be defined and this measure should either be sufficiently comprehensive to cover the entire contribution of each member or be accepted as a surrogate measure of their contributions if it is less than comprehensive of their total contribution.

Second, agreement must be reached on the scale of contributions appropriate for a re-distributed burden. Should contributions be proportionate, and if so, to what should they be proportionate? Should they be disproportionate, and if so, by how much?

There is general agreement that defence expenditures as a proportion of GNP (the D/GNP ratio) is the best available measure of a country's defence burden: MOD (1976), Benoit & Lubell (1960), Benoit (1973), Russett (1964), Olson & Zeckhauser (1968), De Strihou (1968), Labour Party (1977). While the D/GNP ratio does not capture the total defence effort—it misses the resource cost of defence—it is a useful surrogate measure of the burden.

On proportion there is bound to be less unanimity. One way to handle this issue is to observe how members behave in respect of their own taxation policies. The main choice is between proportion (all members with the same D/GNP ratio), disproportion (the D/GNP rising with income), and progressivity.

De Strihou's method

De Strihou (1968) (see also Rosenstein–Rodan 1961; Pincus 1965; Kravis & Davenport 1963) devised an interesting method of applying ability-to-pay criteria to burden sharing in NATO for 1963 and, by putting new wine in an old model, I will apply his method to data for 1975.

The method of calculation is fairly simple. Britain's progressive taxation net of benefits schedule is used to determine NATO members' defence burdens taking account of their per capita incomes as the criterion for their ability to pay. The members are ranked by their per capita incomes around the NATO average, and the net tax rates from the progressivity schedule are applied to these rankings. This treats the NATO members as a group of individuals whose per capita incomes differ from the group average, as if they were a group of taxpayers in Britain whose incomes differ from the national average, and taxes them accordingly.

Having established the net tax rate that would be applied to NATO members if they were on the British progressivity schedule the next step is to adjust this rate according to their actual defence contributions (D/GNP). This is done by dividing the net tax rate by their D/GNP. Taking each member in turn the resultant coefficient is divided into all the other member's D/GNP ratios which provides a column of adjusted D/GNPs assuming that the standard member's D/GNP ratio is appropriate, given its per capita income.

Before looking at the results it is necessary to enter a few caveats, which are easier to mention than to overcome. There is the usual problem of conversion of national currencies into a common currency. Official exchange rates are unlikely to reflect real comparability of costs and with shifting rates which one is to be chosen?

There is the problem of the dispersion of per capita incomes in the group which might lead to bias in the progressivity schedule at either end of the scale. But perhaps the most serious problem arises from the distribution of incomes within member countries. The method uses average per capita income which might be unrepresentative of actual per capita incomes in the population. Low income countries may be assessed at a rate of tax for the burden-sharing exercise which enables the better-off individuals in that country to be treated more favourably than similar individuals in a high income country. This breaches the equal treatment for equals principle. De Strihou reduced this problem by excluding the low per capita income members, Turkey, Portugal, Greece and Italy. Kravis & Davenport (1963) following Rosenstein–Rodan (1961) tackled the problem by estimating a world distribution of income using binary comparisons between America and foreign income distributions (Pincus 1965).

The relative differences between NATO per capita incomes will vary according to the price weights used. The richer a country is the more the exchange rate will overstate its real income due to the higher relative price of services which are not justified by relative productivities, for example. American price weights raise European incomes nearer to American levels and European price weights lower them (Gilbert & Associates 1957; Kravis & Davenport 1963; De Strihou 1968). None of these problems totally discredit the method, although they would call for fine tuning in a serious application of it.

Table 5.1 British taxation net of benefits schedule, 1975

Range of original income	Average original income	Taxes	Benefits	Income net of taxes & benefits	As % of original income	British net tax rate
£	£	£	£	£		
816–1193	1005	467	1662	2200	219	−119
1194–1748	1471	516	1363	2318	158	−58
1749–2560	2155	793	960	2322	108	−8
2561–3749	3155	1180	898	2873	91	9
3750–5489	4620	1687	902	3835	83	17
5490–8037	6764	2510	883	5137	76	24

Average income £3195

Source: CSO (1977), extracted and re-arranged

The British taxation net of benefits schedule for 1975 is shown in Table 5.1. This shows the British Net Tax Rate for incomes in the range £816 to £8037. Average income from the table (unweighted) is £3195. In Table 5.2 the per capita incomes of NATO members in US dollars for 1975 are shown and the average NATO income is $4610.9. Each country's per capita income is shown in column 2 as a proportion of the NATO average.

The arithmetical calculation is as follows, using Germany as an example. Germany's per capita income of $6409 is 139 per cent of the NATO average of $4610. If Germany was an individual in Britain under British tax liabilities what income would it receive if it had an income 139 per cent of the British average of £3195? This would be £4441 which is in the range £3750 to £5489. The British net tax rate in that range is at a maximum of 17 per cent and to find what it would be for an

Table 5.2 Per capita income in US dollars, 1975

Country	Per capita income ($)	As proportion of NATO average (%)
Germany	6409	139·00
Denmark	6395	138·69
Norway	6389	138·56
America	6351	137·74
Belgium	6231	135·14
Canada	5739	124·47
Netherlands	5570	120·80
France	5521	119·74
Britain	3725	80·79
Italy	2959	64·17
Greece	2354	51·05
Portugal	1602	34·74
Turkey	696	15·09
Average	4610·9	

Source: MOD (1976)

income of £4441, the difference between the average for that range (£4620) and the average for the range below it (£3155) is divided by the difference between the tax rate in the upper range (17 per cent) and the tax rate in the lower range (9 per cent) which is 8, and this produces a figure of £183·13 as the per unit tax rate change. The average income of £4441 is below the average for the range (£4620) by £178·6 and dividing this difference by £183·13 produces 0·98 which has to be deducted from the 17 per cent tax rate to give the net tax rate on the German average income of 16·02.

The arithmetic is fairly simple if tedious but if each country is treated in this way the NATO Net Tax Rate for each country on the British progressivity schedule given its relative per capita income can be calculated as in column 1 of Table 5.3.

There are nine columns numbered in the table and each one represents the calculation of the members' D/GNP ratio assuming that the D/GNP ratio of one of the members is appropriate (identified by starred D/GNP which can be read from the row). For example column 1 takes Germany's D/GNP of 4·42 per cent (which includes its contribution to the defence of

Table 5·3 Percentage of GNP to be spent on defence using British tax progression as the criterion for burden sharing, 1975

NATO net tax rate	Member	1	2	3	4	5	6	7	8	9
16·02	1 Germany	4·42•	2·25	3·15	6·02	3·08	2·57	4·45	4·92	13·43
15·97	2 Denmark	4·41	2·24•	3·14	6·00	3·07	2·56	4·44	4·91	13·49
15·95	3 Norway	4·41	2·24	3·14•	6·00	3·07	2·56	4·43	4·90	13·37
15·80	4 America	4·36	2·22	3·11	5·94•	3·04	2·53	4·39	4·85	13·24
15·45	5 Belgium	4·27	2·17	3·04	5·81	2·97•	2·48	4·29	4·75	12·95
13·48	6 Canada	3·72	1·89	2·65	5·07	2·59	2·16•	3·75	4·14	11·30
12·85	7 Netherlands	3·55	1·80	2·58	4·83	2·47	2·06	3·57•	3·95	10·77
12·66	8 France	3·50	1·78	2·49	4·76	2·43	2·03	3·52	3·89•	10·61
5·87	9 Britain	1·62	0·82	1·16	2·21	1·13	0·94	1·63	1·80	4·92•

Sources: calculated from GNP and defence data in IISS (1977); De Strihou (1968)
• actual D/GNP concerted for calculation into US dollars

Berlin) as being a correct allocation. The ratio of the NATO tax rate of 16·02 and the D/GNP is calculated (= 3·62) and then each member's tax rate is divided by this ratio to identify what their D/GNP ratios would be if Germany's was correct at 4·42 per cent of GNP allocated to defence. As Germany has a per capita income of 139 per cent of the average NATO income it follows that the other members will have a lower D/GNP in these circumstances because their per capita incomes are lower than Germany's. This situation would be satisfactory from an equity point of view if ability to pay is an appropriate criterion for burden sharing.

There are some interesting results from this exercise identified in Table 5.3. For instance, Britain's current D/GNP ratio of 4·92, given its relatively low per capita income in NATO (80 per cent of the NATO average), is shown to be too high on the basis of applying its own progressivity schedule to NATO members' defence burdens. In seven cases its D/GNP ratio would fall to below 2 per cent if what other members are contributing to defence was their fair share. In the case of America being the standard (column 4) Britain's share would only be 2·21 per cent or less than half of its actual D/GNP. This can be dramatically underlined by taking Britain's D/GNP (column 9) as the standard in which case, given their relative abilities to pay, the other members would be spending proportions of their GNP in excess of 10 per cent.

If America's D/GNP ratio of 5·94 per cent is taken as the standard (column 4) all the other members, with the exception of Britain in Table 5.3, would be required to increase their defence expenditures above the 1975 levels, with three members, Germany, Denmark and Norway, needing to raise their outlays above America's as a proportion of GNP. On ability-to-pay criteria this is a measure of the inequitable burden sharing in NATO as currently organised. It gives some support to American complaints about burden sharing in NATO (Pincus 1965) and to British views that its own contribution is out of line with those of its European partners (MOD 1975).

In Table 5.4 the D/GNP ratios of column 4 are translated into absolute money amounts. The required and actual ratios

Table 5.4 Proposed NATO allocations to defence using the American 1975 D/GNP ratio as a standard

Country	Required D/GNP	Actual D/GNP	GNP US $b	Defence in US $b	Required defence in US $b
Germany	6·02	4·42	441·6	19·518	26·58
Denmark	6·00	2·24	41·9	0·939	2·51
Norway	6·00	3·14	29·6	0·929	1·78
America	5·94	5·94	1498·0	88·98	88·98
Belgium	5·81	2·97	66·4	1·97	3·86
Canada	5·07	2·16	137·0	2·96	6·95
Netherlands	4·83	3·57	83·4	2·97	4·03
France	4·76	3·89	359·0	13·98	17·09
Britain	2·21	4·92	226·0	11·12	4·99
Total				143·34	151·77
Members not included above				8·64	
Total NATO defence expenditure				151·98	

Sources: GNP: IISS (1976); D/GNP: Table 5.3

are applied to each country's GNP and shown in US dollars. Actual defence expenditures of the members in the table total $143 billion and when the contributions of the members not listed in Tables 5.3 and 5.4 are added ($8 billion) the total expenditure of NATO on defence in 1975 was $151 billion. (The absence of the poorer NATO members is explained by the effect of the British progressivity schedule on them; they would in fact be net receivers of payments rather than contributors using this type of criterion, as their per capita incomes are so much lower than the NATO average.)

When the required defence expenditure is aggregated it adds up to $151 billion largely because most members would have their defence contributions increased and total NATO expenditures would rise. This provides some evidence for the suboptimal provision of the alliance suggested by the Olson & Zeckhauser model (1968). This additional amount could in fact pay for the defence efforts of the poorer NATO members by some form of transfer payment to them which is an arithmetical confirmation of the implications of a progressivity schedule. Of course, this presentation takes no account of the political implications of such a suggestion.

Though most of the members in the table would have their defence expenditures increased, Britain would have its reduced from $11 billion to $5 billion. This reflects the relative per capita income position of Britain in respect of its European and North American partners. There are serious implications that follow from such a proposal and these will be discussed in a later chapter.

Table 5.5 The effect of proportionality as a criterion for burden sharing by use of members' share of total NATO GNP (1976)

Country	GNP	% NATO	Actual defence expen- diture	% NATO	Defence expenditure when pro- portional to NATO GNP	Propor- tional D/GNP	Actual D/GNP
	(1)	(2)	(3)	(4)	(5)	(6)	(7)
	US $b	%	US $b	%	US $b	%	%
America	1692·4	50·05	102·910	62·70	82·05	4·9	6·0
Germany	449·1	13·39	18·758	11·44	21·92	4·9	4·2
France	353·2	10·55	12·857	7·8	17·24	4·9	3·7
Britain	224·5	6·69	10·734	6·55	10·953	4·9	4·8
Italy	161·6	4·82	3·821	2·33	7·892	4·9	2·6
Canada	175·3	5·23	3·231	1·97	8·563	4·9	1·9
Netherlands	85·1	2·54	2·825	1·72	4·159	4·9	3·4
Belgium	66·5	1·98	2·013	1·23	3·242	4·9	3·0
Turkey	40·2	1·2	2·800	1·71	1·964	4·9	5·6
Denmark	34·2	1·02	0·861	0·53	1·67	4·9	2·8
Norway	31·1	0·93	0·902	0·55	1·523	4·9	3·1
Greece	22·6	0·67	1·249	0·76	1·097	4·9	5·5
Portugal	15·8	0·47	0·748	0·46	0·770	4·9	3·9
Luxembourg	2·4	0·07	0·023	0·0001	0·115	4·9	1·2
Totals	3354		163·733		163·06		

Sources: GNP and defence expenditure from IISS (1977)

Finally, it is worth looking at the effect of a strictly proportional criterion for burden sharing, and this is illustrated in Table 5.5. In a proportional system members would pay for defence in proportion to the size of their GNP irrespective of their per capita incomes. The degree of proportionality has still to be settled and several alternatives exist. The one illustrated in Table 5.5 is a system whereby members pay for defence in proportion to their shares of NATO GNP (column 2). If these shares are compared with the shares of their actual defence expenditure in total NATO defence expenditure (column 4) the discrepancies can be seen. America contributes 62 per cent of the NATO defence expenditure yet accounts for 50 per cent of NATO GNP. Turkey and Greece marginally exceed their GNP shares but others, notably Canada, France, Italy, Denmark and tiny Luxembourg fall well short of their shares using this criterion. When this criterion is used the D/GNP ratio appears as 4·9 per cent. Applying this ratio across the alliance would produce $163 billion for defence expenditure by reallocating the burden among the members.

The problem with the proportionality criterion is its non-progressive nature. The smaller GNP countries pay the same proportion of their incomes as the richer GNP countries irrespective of per capita incomes. Italy's per capita income is about half that of Canada's but its defence allocation is almost the same. Britain's per capita income (Table 5.2) is less than that of Canada's but it is assigned a higher defence contribution. These kinds of anomolies breach the equal circumstances principle—a man with the same income as another man but with a family to support ought not to pay the same income tax, nor should a country with a higher population to support out of its GNP.

A proportional system is regarded as being less equitable than a progressive system. Members contribute the same D/GNP but differing absolute amounts. There is in practice a positive relationship between the amount spent on defence and the size of the GNP (Knorr 1970; and see Table 3.5) but not a positive relationship between D/GNP and GNP. A preference for progressivity implies an acceptance of disproportionality which, though predicted by the Olson & Zeckhauser model, does not appear to be produced by the alliance on its own account. This implies a need for considered intervention to bring about what is preferred on equity grounds. The next chapter examines the history of attempts to achieve equity in cost sharing in some international organisations, including NATO.

6

Some International Cost-sharing Arrangements

No general solution of the cost-sharing problem has yet been devised. In its place there are a number of partial, and sometimes purely expedient, solutions operated in different circumstances for different purposes. The main features of some of these arrangements are the subject of this chapter. I will begin with non-defence organisations and complete the selective survey with NATO's own headquarters and infrastructure arrangements.

International governmental agencies

The most prolific type of international organisation is associated with one aspect or another of preserving or promoting internationally workable arrangements for the conduct of relations between countries. Some of these agencies are represented in Table 6.1. The oldest in the table is the Universal Postal Union (UPU) which was founded in 1874. The most recent is the European Economic Community (1958) which expanded in 1972 and may expand again in 1980. The difference in size of budget and scope of purpose between these organisations has itself produced differences in cost-sharing arrangements but has by no means made the subject any less important.

The UPU governs regulations for international postal movements (Reinsch 1916) and bases members' contributions on a version of the benefit approach. Countries join the UPU because they see some benefit in doing so and that benefit —access to a well-ordered and regulated international postal system—can roughly be measured by the use a country makes of the postal system. Members are divided into seven bands depending on the numerical size of their population (potential addressees), the extent of their national territory (size of the postal system as an organisation) and the volume of transactions (density of use of the system). Each band is assessed a number of units and the annual budget is divided into units which are then assigned to each member according to the units in its band. There is an upper limit set on any member's contribution which must not exceed 4·18 per cent of the total cost of the UPU. Members are permitted to move to a higher band if they wish and apparently some of them take this as a matter of national pride and opt to contribute more in this way. A willingness to contribute more in these circumstances ought not to be discounted as it happens in other cases, notably

Table 6.1 Cost apportionments for selected countries to selected international organisations as percentages of total organisation costs

Country	Universal Postal Union (1931)	League of Nations (1935)	United Nations (1961)	UN Specialised Agencies (1962)						
				ILO	FAO	UNESCO	ICAO	WHO	IAEA	IMCO
Argentina	0·55	2·9	1·11	1·42	1·35	1·07	1·20	1·00	1·02	1·09
Australia	2·77	2·7	1·79	1·86	2·22	1·73	2·50	1·62	1·65	0·77
Belgium	1·66	1·8	1·30	1·38	1·61	1·26	1·63	1·18	1·20	0·83
Brazil	1·66	2·9	1·02	1·38	1·38	0·99	1·68	0·92	0·94	
Canada	2·77	3·5	3·11	3·40	4·18	3·01	4·70	2·82	2·87	1·80
China*	2·77	4·6	5·01	2·04		2·50	0·67	4·54	4·62	1·15
Czech/kia	1·66	2·9	0·87	0·92		0·84	0·85	0·79	0·80	
Denmark	1·11	1·2	0·60	0·73	0·78	0·58	0·93	0·54	0·55	1·69
France	2·77	7·9	6·40	6·10	7·96	6·19	7·83	5·80	5·90	3·65
Germany*	2·77	0·7		4·34	7·64	5·16	5·17	4·83	4·91	3·47
Greece	1·66	1·5	0·23	0·21	0·31	0·22	0·27	0·21	0·21	3·38
India	2·77	1·5	2·46	3·07	2·72	2·38	2·56	2·23	2·27	1·41
Ireland	0·55	1·0	0·16	0·24	0·19		0·24	0·14		0·52
Italy	2·77	6·0	2·25	2·37	3·0	2·18	2·43	2·04	2·07	3·76
Japan	2·77	6·0	2·19	2·00	3·04	2·12	2·22	1·98	2·02	5·18
Netherlands	1·66	2·3	1·01	1·16	1·35	0·98	2·51	0·91	0·93	3·09
Norway	1·11	0·9	0·49	0·52	0·60	0·47	0·83	0·44	0·45	6·92
Poland	1·66	3·2	1·37	1·24	1·72	1·32	1·22	1·24	1·26	0·85
Portugal	1·11	0·6	0·20	0·28	0·21					
Spain	3·21	4·0	0·93	1·08	1·15	0·90	1·02	0·84	0·86	1·36
Sweden	1·66	1·8	1·39	1·63	1·74	1·34	1·82	1·26	1·28	2·60
Switzerland	1·66	1·7		1·30	1·27	0·94	1·53	0·88	0·89	0·54
Turkey	1·11	1·0	0·59	0·72	0·54	0·57		1·63	1·66	
UK	2·77	10·5	7·78	9·42	10·15	7·53	9·88	7·05	7·17	12·45
USA	2·77		32·51	25·0	32·02	31·46	32·95	31·71	32·27	15·30
USSR	2·77	7·9	13·62	10·0		13·18		12·34	12·54	4·44

Table 6.1 *continued*

Country	IMF	IBRD	IFC	IDA	OECD (1962)	Council of Europe (1962)	Euratom Admin. (1962)	Research (1962)	EEC Social Fund (1962)
Argentina	1·83	1·80	1·69	1·94					
Australia	2·61	2·57	2·26	2·08					
Belgium	1·66	2·17	2·54		2·90	3·0	7·9	9·9	8·8
Brazil	1·93	1·80	1·18	1·94					
Canada	3·59	3·62	3·67	3·91	4·91				
China*	3·59	3·62		3·13					
Czech/kia	0·85			0·90					
Denmark	0·85	0·84	0·77	0·90	1·33	1·7			
France	5·14	5·07	5·92	5·47	12·88	17·7	28·0	30·0	32·0
Germany†	5·14	5·07	3·72	5·47	14·35	17·7	28·0	30·0	32·0
Greece	0·39	0·24	0·28	0·26	3·0				
India	3·92	3·86	4·51	4·17					
Ireland	0·29	0·29	0·34	0·31	1·1				
Italy	1·76	1·74	2·03	1·87	6·95	17·7	28·0	23·0	20·0
Japan	3·27	3·21	2·82	3·46					
Netherlands	2·69	2·65	3·10	2·86	2·57	4·0	7·9	6·9	7·0
Norway	0·65	0·64	0·56	0·69	1·02	1·3			
Poland									
Portugal	0·39	0·39							
Spain	0·98	0·97	1·13	1·04					
Sweden	0·98	0·97	1·13	1·04	2·82	3·0			
Switzerland					1·26				
Turkey	0·56	0·55	0·48	0·60	2·05	9·0			
UK	12·74	12·54	14·66	13·54	16·29	17·7			
USA	26·95	30·63	35·81	33·06	25·00				
USSR									

Sources: Sumberg 1946; Myers 1935; Singer 1961; Pincus 1965; Stoessinger 1964

* in post-war years refers to Taiwan.

† in post-war years refers to Federal Republic of Germany.

Britain's, in other organisations.

The benefit criterion is a natural choice when a tangible benefit can be estimated or approximated by some indicator such as the amount of postal traffic, or miles of railway track, or passengers carried, and it is most likely to be approved when there are a large number of potential contributors and a small budget. But once the numbers become small and the budget large there are likely to be reservations about the regressive implications of benefit payments and a leaning towards ability-to-pay criteria. It will be seen that most organisations operate a mixture of the two approaches. For example, the imposition of a ceiling or floor on contributions is basically a benefit constraint because it means that everybody pays something and nobody pays the lot.

A low budget does not mean an absence of financial controversy, particularly where the benefits of the organisation are less tangible than those of the UPU. An organisation such as the League of Nations (LoN), which had a small budget and a lot of implicit responsibilities, could be in constant financial crisis. A small sum for contentious purposes can create as much controversy as a large sum for an approved purpose. The LoN's budget was 27 million gold francs annually (or \$5·4 million) (Stoessinger 1964) of which Britain's share at 10 per cent was the largest. Originally, the LoN adopted the UPU's seven band system but abandoned it in 1924 for an ability-to-pay formula which was arrived at by 'subtracting the product of population and minimum per capita income subsistence from the member's gross national income' (Singer 1959). A ceiling on contributions was also introduced in order to limit the contributions required from the low income/high population members India and China (Schelling 1955; Singer 1961).

The shift to ability-to-pay criteria required a more scientific measurement of income, particularly on a comparable basis, and the developments in national income accounting made this more applicable. The complexities of some of the formulae using ability-to-pay criteria, however, owe less to measurement problems than to political expediency.

In 1963 the United Nations (UN) had a budget of about \$500 million and a membership of 104 countries. The per capita income and GNP variation among the membership was, and remains, extremely wide. The Committee on Contributions worked out a formula which can be briefly described to illustrate the UN's broad principles in these matters.

The two key statistics are national income and population. If a country had a per capita income of below \$1000 it had its national income statistic adjusted by taking the difference between its per capita income and \$1000 as a percentage of \$1000, halving it, and then reducing the national income by the halved percentage amount. This reduced national income was the figure to which the assessment (equivalent to a tax) was applied. The formula can be expressed as:

$$\frac{Y_i\,[1-0\cdot5(\$1000-\bar{Y}_i/\$1000)]}{\Sigma Y_i\,\{[1-0\cdot5\,(\$1000-\bar{Y}_i/\$1000)]\}}$$

where Y_i is the national income of country i and $\bar{Y}_i$ is the national income per capita (Kravis & Davenport 1963; Stoessinger 1964; Pincus 1965). Those countries with per capita incomes in excess of \$1000 did not get any reduction in their taxable GNP. A ceiling of 30 per cent of the total cost of the UN was fixed on any single member's assessment (which so far only affects the United States) and a floor of 0·04 per cent was introduced (which so far affects about a third of the members) (Padelford 1963). A further rule was applied that where a member's contribution per capita exceeded that of the largest contributor (i.e. America) its percentage contribution was reduced to the point where the per capita contributions were equalised. This rule has so far only benefited Canada.

In the UN cost-sharing arrangement the richest members are the largest contributors. America contributes a third of the UN budget and had to fight hard to avoid having to pay a half or more of it when the UN was founded. The five permanent members of the security council, America, Russia, Britain, France and China, contribute two-thirds of the budget and in all 20 per cent of the membership contribute 90 per cent of the total (Stoessinger 1964).

The International Labour Organisation (ILO) was taken over by the UN from the LoN and this probably explains America's relatively low contribution at 25 per cent of the budget compared to its UN assessments. Nevertheless, this still made it the major contributor and when, after many years of domestic agitation, America withdrew from the ILO in 1977 it represented a major financial blow to the organisation. (Russia had left the ILO in 1939 and re-joined in 1954 for similar political reasons—it did not agree with the use its critics made of the organisation.) There is a broad correlation between contributions and ability to pay probably tempered with political sensitivity.

The other agencies of the UN (see Table 6.1) follow broadly the same cost-sharing policy. This results in a few members contributing the bulk of the funds. America and Britain contribute 42 per cent of the funds of the UN Food and Agriculture Organisation (FAO) and with Russia contribute over half of the UN Educational, Scientific and Cultural Organisation (UNESCO), the World Health Organisation (WHO), and the International Atomic Energy Authority (IAEA). In some of the smaller agencies the pattern while repeated is not so marked. The International Civil Aviation Organisation (ICAO) uses an ability-to-pay formula for 75 per cent of its budget and a surrogate benefit formula based on the 'interest and importance of civil aviation' to the member for the remaining 25 per cent. This is possible because in this case something can be measured as a benefit, and also because the major civil aviation members are also among the richer members of the UN. The Intergovernmental Maritime Consultative Organisation (IMCO) is likewise well placed to apply a mixture of both criteria because both benefit and ability to pay are closely correlated.

The International Monetary Fund (IMF) and the International Bank for Reconstruction and Development (IBRD) have an elaborate cost-sharing formula based on ability to pay but also largely influenced by a member's perception of national prestige. The Fund's resources were available in the form of quotas which members could draw on in periods of economic difficulty much in the manner of a bank overdraft. The size of a member's quota reflected international perceptions of creditworthiness and importance in the world economy (much as an individual's access to overdraft facilities at the local bank reflects the manager's professional judgment as to his creditworthiness).

The quotas were calculated using the following indicators: 2 per cent of the 1940 national income; 5 per cent of the gold and dollar holdings of July 1943; 10 per cent of the average annual imports for 1934–8 and 10 per cent of the maximum variation in annual exports for the same period. All these were then multiplied by 1 plus the ratio of the average annual exports (1934–8) to national income. Those countries which were major international trading economies would have the largest quotas. As voting in the IMF was to be in proportion to the size of the quota it might pay a country to try to get a higher quota. America's was fixed at twice that of Britain and all other countries were to be pro rata to Britain's. The ability-to-pay criterion was present in the form of the national income but this was skilfully combined with a benefit element in the form of a member's importance in world trade, it being expected that the major traders would probably need greater access to funds than minor traders.

The IBRD formula was based on similar considerations to the IMF's. The formula was 4 per cent of a country's national income and 6 per cent of its average annual foreign trade for 1934–8 with up to a further 20 per cent of the quota open to negotiation and political arm twisting (Sumberg 1946; Pincus 1965). Being a bank the IBRD is under less financial pressure in raising its budgets since it has an income from its operations, as does the International Finance Corporation (IFC). In all three organisations Britain has a major allocation (Table 6.1) and to a great extent this reflects its political pride more than its ability to pay.

The International Development Association (IDA) raises funds to replenish its low-interest grants to developing countries. Members pay their quotas in two distinct ways. One group of richer members pay most of their quotas in hard currencies and the other group of poorer members can pay up to 90 per cent of their quotas in local currency. The European and North American contributions account for over 67 per cent of the total collected.

The Organisation of Economic Co-operation and Development (OECD) carried over the financial practice of its predecessor the Organisation for European Economic Co-operation (OEEC) which involved a unanimity rule in cost-sharing its main budget. The sum involved was relatively small ($5.5 million a year), and four members, America (25 per cent), Britain (16 per cent) Germany (14 per cent) and France (12 per cent), dominate the budget allocation. The OECD specified that expenditures other than the administrative budget would be apportioned 'on such basis as the Council may decide' (Stoessinger 1964).

The Council of Europe (CoE) has allocated its budget contributions among members on what appear to be political rather than economic grounds. That Germany, France and Britain should contribute roughly comparable amounts would be supported on GNP grounds, but Italy is assessed for the same amount (17·7 per cent) which is at variance with its relative GNP and certainly with its relative per capita GNP. This is the more striking in the case of Turkey which is assessed at 9 per cent of the total budget though among the poorest of the members (for example it is assessed three times more than Sweden). As the purposes of the CoE are extremely vague (though it has contributed a flag design for a United Europe which may or may not eventually come to pass) it is surprising that such economic anomalies are accepted.

Lastly, the original six members of the European Economic Community (EEC) in the two examples shown in Table 6.1 show the pattern followed in the early years of the organisation. Germany and France being the largest in GNP paid the most, followed by Italy and then the others. This was not apparently influenced by per capita incomes. Italy probably concurred in such arrangements because of the strongly pro-European unity policies across its political spectrum. Given that voting is weighted to contributions this also gave Italy a greater influence in the development of the EEC and its agencies than it might otherwise have merited if it had chosen a strict ability-to-pay formula.

The proposals for a New International Economic Order that have been put forward by the UN Conference on Trade and Development (UNCTAD) have also had cost-sharing implications (UN 1974; Morton & Tulloch 1977). Similar implications have also appeared in other UN agency proposals. The major element of these proposals is the resolution of the ability-to-pay and benefit approaches for an organisation that embraces identifiable members in great need (beneficiaries of change) and identifiable members with great means (beneficiaries of the status quo). The avowed purpose of UN sponsored programmes is intervention to change current arrangements. The essential problem is that the gainers cannot afford to undertake these programmes without the active support of the losers who are not willing to make the changes.

Cost-sharing proposals in this environment are likely to involve ability to pay with some weighting for benefit, the latter usually applied in both directions, i.e. to the tangible beneficiaries who gain from the change and to those others who do not gain directly—indeed they may 'lose'—but are believed to gain intangibly from a 'better' world distribution of income between the rich (themselves) and the poor.

An example of this type of proposal can be seen in a FAO proposed policy for dealing with world cereal stocks for a food security policy in 1975. Countries were to maintain certain stocks of cereals financed by themselves at a target level chosen by themselves. This might (and probably would) result in the world stocks being below the desired stocks for food security. The FAO proposed that the shortfall in stocks be made up by international action and that the costs of financing the additional stocks should be allocated among the countries concerned on a cost-sharing basis. While the actual cost-sharing formula was not specified it was agreed it would cover some or all of the following indicators:

1. GDP or GDP per capita ('stocks would be financed by those countries in the best economic and financial position to do so')
2. Variability in production ('countries most vulnerable to production fluctuations make larger demands on the world reserves')
3. Relative shares in world grain production
4. Relative consumption levels of cereals ('increases the share of some importing countries')
5. Importance of countries in world cereals trade, or
6. Some weighted combination of all or some of such criteria (FAO 1975)

Item 1 is a straight ability-to-pay criterion while items 2 to 5 involve an identification of benefits. The committee were realistic enough to note that 'in practice, the pattern of cost sharing, although likely to be related to some of these criteria, would in the final analysis have to be determined through negotiations between the participating countries' (FAO 1975,

p. 8). Items 1, 3 and 5 might weight the burden towards the richer countries (America, Canada and Australia) while items 2 and 4 might weight it towards the poorer importers most in need of a policy on world food security. These considerations would be important in the attitude of the negotiators to specific cost-sharing formulae.

The general conclusions from this brief survey can now be summarised. Benefit criteria on their own have very limited application and can only be used in international cost sharing when specific benefits can be identified and located in each participating country. In international organisations where there are wide disparities in per capita incomes or GNP the ability-to-pay criteria are likely to be modified by floors or ceilings on contributions in order to maintain some connection between benefit and share of the burden of provision. In international organisations where there are both tangible and intangible benefits and where the purposes of the organisation are to change the status quo at tangible cost to some of the participants, ability-to-pay criteria will also be modified by some consideration of the benefits and some assessment according to interests. The former will tend to weaken ability to pay as a criterion and the latter will tend to reinforce it where the 'losers' are also the richer members. In international organisations where the income differences are relatively small for some of the members the equity consideration of equal treatment for equals will be adopted and individual members will tend to accept higher assessments than strict equity would require in order to gain political or prestige advantages.

Cost-sharing programmes in NATO

Each member of NATO has a responsibility to equip and maintain its own national forces. This has not prevented, and indeed has possibly encouraged, international co-operation between the members on joint military procurement programmes. A multitude of non-interoperable equipment in the field presents its own problems of military management. Modest advances have been and are being made in the area of joint procurement but there is a long way to go before the kind of common procurement that is experienced in the Warsaw Pact (WARPAC) countries is achieved in NATO.

NATO has made some progress in the area of military infrastructure by persuading individual members to contribute to these programmes on the basis of cost-sharing formulae. The infrastructure programme (Slices II to XXIV and Slice I in Germany and the European Development Improvement Programme, EDIP) totalled 2359 million Infrastructure Accounting Units which in 1967 (pre-devaluation) pounds sterling equalled £2·359 billion. This was about 2 per cent of a single year's military budget spread over twenty years. In other words the amount involved was relatively small.

In Table 6.2 details of the percentage allocations to members for these type of programmes are given along with the 1962 headquarters allocation. The formula is based on three main criteria: 'the contributive capacity of the member country, the advantage accruing to the user countries and the

Table 6.2 NATO infrastructure and headquarters allocations as percentages of total costs 1950–70

Member	I (1950)•	Infrastructure Slice numbers: II–VII (1960)	VIII–XI (1957)	XII–XV (1966)	XVI–XX (1966)	XXI–XXV (1970)	Headquarters (1962) †	Defence expenditure as % of total NATO expenditure (1970)
America		43·679	36·98	30·85	25·77	26·6716	24·20	74·2
Germany‡			13·72	20·00	21·86	25·1767	16·10	6·0
France§	45·46	15·041	11·87	12·00	13·16		17·10	5·8
Britain	27·27	12·758	9·88	10·50	10·42	11·9950	19·50	5·8
Canada		6·021	6·15	5·15	5·48	6·3132	5·08	1·9
Italy		5·681	5·61	5·97	6·58	7·5757	5·96	2·5
Netherlands	13·64	3·889	3·51	3·83	4·23	4·8738	2·85	1·1
Belgium	13·88	5·462	4·39	4·24	4·61	5·3031	2·86	0·7
Turkey		1·371	1·75	1·10	1·10	1·2626	1·65	0·5
Denmark		2·767	2·63	2·87	3·07	3·5354	1·65	0·4
Norway		2·280	2·19	2·37	2·59	2·9798	1·15	0·4
Greece		0·750	0·87	0·67	0·66	0·7676	0·39	0·4
Portugal		0·146	0·28	0·28	0·31	0·3535	0·65	0·4
Luxembourg	0·45	0·155	0·17	0·17	0·18	0·2020	0·09	0·008

Sources: NATO 1974; Pincus 1965; IISS 1971
• Brussels Treaty Powers
† including an assessment for Iceland, which does not have national defence forces, of 0·05% or $3690
‡ paid 50% of Programme Slice VIIb, not shown
§ France withdrew from integrated NATO activities in 1966

economic benefit to the host country' (NATO 1976a). In the case of the headquarters contributions these are claimed to be based strictly on ability-to-pay criteria (Pincus 1965), and it therefore affords a useful comparison with the infrastructure programme slices which are weighted with some benefit criteria.

The main projects to which the infrastructure programmes have been allocated include building airfields (over 220 of them), constructing a communications system (50 000 kilometres of landlines, radio links and submarine cables), laying down a 10 000 kilometre pipeline system for fuel and a 2 million cubic metre storage facility, and installing the NATO Air Defence Ground Environment (NADGE) early-warning and fighter-control system.

The system operates as follows. Proposals for infrastructure projects are considered by NATO committees and if approved are implemented by the country which will host the facility. NATO does not administer the funds but acts as a secretarial body recording the transactions. Payments are made direct to the host country according to the agreed cost-sharing formula. The host country is responsible on its own account for acquiring suitable sites, though this is less of an economic cost than a budget cost because acquisition costs are normally a transfer from the nation's tax payers to other citizens. The project is regularly inspected and the accounts audited by non-host country specialists to ensure progress in construction and probity in the claims made on other members for funds.

Olson & Zeckhauser (1968) predicted that the 'larger members of an alliance would bear a smaller share of the infrastructure burden than of the main alliance burdens' (p. 276). As already noted, by 'larger' they mean larger in size of GNP. Their argument in favour of the proposition is based on the differences between assigned contributions to marginal units of a common output and national contributions which cover the full cost of national provision. Infrastructure costs are shared according to a formula which is agreed by the members; national costs are not. In the last column of Table 6.2 defence expenditures of the members for 1970 as a percentage of total NATO defence expenditure are shown. The difference between these shares and the cost-sharing percentages is striking.

America's cost-sharing percentage has been declining from 43 per cent to 26 per cent of infrastructure costs while its 1970 share of NATO expenditures was 74 per cent (this share declined to 62 per cent by 1976). Most of the other European members had infrastructure shares greatly in excess of their national shares of the NATO total defence effort.

The cost-sharing formula adopted by NATO takes account of ability to pay in the contributive capacity of the member as measured by its national income. This is weighted by a benefit assessment. The beneficiary can be identified in the use made by a member of the facility, thus, for example, the British Royal Air Force using NATO-built airfields in Germany would be assigned a share of the costs over and above its national income share. The other beneficiary is the host country through the economic spin-offs from construction and funding. These are in effect private benefits from the provision of the public good and therefore must be allowed for in covering the cost of the installations. Foreign exchange inflows from members' contributions of their cost shares, employment of local labour, improvements to the local transport system and access to facilities, such as pipelines, benefit the local economy. If the installations, for example the RAF airfields in Germany, benefit the German economy, then the German people should be assessed a contribution which takes this into account. In Programme Slice VIIb Germany paid 50 per cent of the cost outright for this reason (NATO 1976a, p. 153). In Table 6.2 it can be seen that Germany has been gradually increasing its contribution from 13 per cent to 25 per cent which is almost the same as America's in 1970. The benefit criteria was weighting Germany's contribution enough to equalise it with what would be largely the ability-to-pay criteria applied to America.

The cost-sharing agreements identified in Table 6.2 did not come about because of the willing acceptance by members of their responsibilities. Programme Slice I was paid for by Britain, France and the Benelux members after a negotiation rather than a specific formula. Similarly Programme Slices II and III were allocated by discussion and bargaining. Lord Ismay, NATO's first Secretary-General, in a candid revelation described the negotiation-cum-formula approach used for the Programme Slice IV agreement:

> They dumped the whole problem in my lap, so I called in three assistant secretaries general, and each of us drew up our list of what we thought the percentage sharing should be, and then we averaged them out. I couldn't for the life of me possibly say on what basis I acted except I tried to take into account all sorts of things like the ability to pay and whether the building would be going on in a country so that it would benefit from the construction and the money spent.
>
> Then we got into the Council meeting in April of 1953, and everybody around the table thought it was a jolly good distribution except for his own, which they thought was too high. Anyway, we went round the table and finally got agreement of each to take what was given within 1·8 per cent of the total, and then we simply divided up that 1·8 per cent among the fourteen, and that's all there was to it. That's why all the shares are in those funny percentage amounts. (Warburton & Wood n.d., quoted in Stoessinger 1964, p. 57)

The shares agreed by this method for Programme Slice IV were: America, 42·86; France, 13·75; Britain, 11·45; Canada, 7·13; Italy, 6·50; Netherlands, 4·07; Belgium, 5·09; Turkey, 2·03; Denmark, 3·05; Norway, 2·54; Greece, 1·01; Portugal, 0·32 and Luxembourg, 0·20 per cent.

The willingness to accept cost shares after negotiation which exceed the national share in NATO's efforts is assisted by the relatively small amounts involved, the specificity of the programmes, the strict accountability of the operations in the host countries, the manifest alliance benefit from having proper facilities, the recognition that direct beneficiaries will contribute more than indirect beneficiaries and the political advantage from co-operation of this kind. Beneficiaries contribute more because even at higher assigned contributions they are still getting installations and facilities built on the home territory at a lower cost because of the contributions of the other members. Private benefits still exceed national costs if other members also contribute.

The important question that arises at this stage is whether it would be possible to devise more ambitious cost-sharing arrangements for other parts of the NATO defence effort and whether there are economic arguments in favour of doing so.

7

Reallocating the Defence Burden among the NATO Allies

Economics can make at least one positive contribution to a debate on burden sharing: it can sort out some of the implications of the various options. If, on equity grounds, the burden of common defence is shared unfairly the question that follows is: What, if anything, should or could be done about it? This must be taken in two parts: Who should actually *do* what, and who should *pay* for it being done? The doers and the payers need not be the same. NATO members could reallocate military tasks between themselves relieving certain members of a resource burden in providing military forces and the associated budgetary burden of raising revenue to pay for them. On efficiency grounds it might be preferable to continue with the current distribution of military functions but reallocate the financial provision among the members so that Britain, say, would continue providing its relatively large defence contribution to NATO and would receive a financial contribution from NATO members for doing so. It is possible for a combination of both changes to take place. In this chapter I discuss some of the economic issues involved, and some of the practical obstacles to changes of this kind.

Sandler's model

If equity is an objective intervention will be required. Olson & Zeckhauser's prediction of disproportionality in an alliance, which would be preferred on equity grounds, does not appear to come about by normal processes. The allocation of the burden in NATO can be shown to be inequitable, at least on the progressivity schedule used by Britain. Intervention is needed to bring about what the Olson & Zeckhauser model predicts will happen but does not.

NATO is an alliance of sovereign and independent states and is not a supranational authority which can intervene in the affairs of member states—in fact one of the reasons for founding NATO was in order to protect the sovereignty of the member states from outside intervention. Therefore proposals for intervention to reallocate defence burdens must secure the support of the members if they are to be implemented. No member can impose a solution to the problem of burden sharing, apart from withdrawing from the organisation. The practical proposals which would secure such support will not be considered in this book. My purpose in this chapter is to examine the theoretical case for reallocation and the implications that follow from it, and I will make cursory references to practical obstacles to implementation.

Sandler (1975) made a most interesting contribution to alliance economics in an extension and revision of the basic Olson & Zeckhauser (1968) model. He explicitly introduced private and public good trade-offs into his model (the income effect noted by De Strihou 1968) and Pareto efficiency movements. This enabled him to discuss tax transfer schemes between alliance members as a solution to sub-optimal resource allocation in defence.

A 'modified Edgeworth box' diagram is used as shown in Figure 7.1. A close examination of the figure will suggest that it is in effect similar to De Strihou's model except that there are two of them, with one turned upside down. There are two allies, two goods, defence (public) and non-defence (private), identical production processes but different linearly homogeneous production functions and a social welfare function through which the citizens reveal their preferences in a community indifference map (compare with Figure 2.4).

Defence is measured along the horizontal axis, OM for country I and $O'K$ for country II, and non-defence on the vertical axis, OP for country I and $O'P$ for country II. PM is the production possibility curve for country I and PK is the same for country II. Equilibrium will occur where the country's

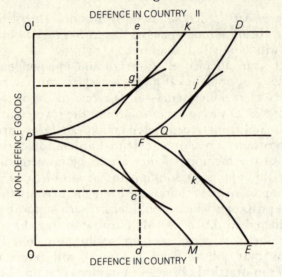

Figure 7.1

community indifference curve is tangential to a point on its production possibility curve. At these points, c and g respectively, there is an equality between the marginal rate of transformation in production and the marginal rate of substitution in consumption between defence and non-defence goods.

In alliance the amount of defence available to one member is its own defence and the defence output of its partner. If country II produces $O'e$ defence, country I's defence availability will increase by that amount from spillovers to OE (where $ME = O'e$). This can be represented in the figure by an outward movement of its production possibility curve PM to FE. Similarly, the defence output of country I, Od, is available now for country II and this moves its production possibility frontier outwards to QD (where $KD = Od$). The new points of tangency, k and j, with the community indifference curves represent new consumption possibilities for the two countries. These need not be final equilibrium positions as the new consumption possibilities and production decisions are influenced by the defence outlays of the alliance partner. Reaction curves as in Olson & Zeckhauser's model (Figure 2.2) will help determine

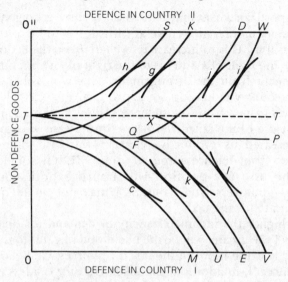

Figure 7.2

final equilibrium though this need not be a Pareto optimum because it may not be a point of tangency for both parties simultaneously. If this is the case there is a possibility of a tax-transfer arrangement which will bring it about.

In Figure 7.2 the tax transfer arrangement is illustrated. The tax shifts resources from one country to another. If resources flow from country II to country I the production possibility frontier will move from *PM* to *TU* (outwards) and from *PK* to *TS* (inwards). Country I now has more resources available for defence and non-defence and country II has less. The total amount of non-defence (private) goods available to both parties is the same but the distribution is now different (*OT* for country I and *O"T* for country II).

Country I will use the additional resources to expand defence output (assuming defence is not an inferior good) and because defence in the alliance is a public good this will increase country II's consumption of defence. Country I's post-tax consumption possibility curve is now tangential to a community indifference curve at *l* which is to the right of *k*. Country II's post-tax consumption possibility curve is tangential to a community indifference curve at i which has to be to the right of j if country II is to increase its welfare from the tax transfer. If l is to the right of k and i is to the right of j then both countries benefit from the arrangement. This is possible because though country II has lost some productive capacity from the tax it has gained from the defence spillovers from country I's efficient use of the taxed resources. In the case of country I it has increased its productive capacity but lost some of the spillovers from defence output in country II. It is not inevitable that the post-tax position will improve both countries' welfare—spillovers from country I may not be adequate to compensate for the tax.

The higher the income elasticity of demand for defence in country I the greater will be the likelihood of gains to the taxed country because more of the taxed resources will be allocated to defence. If, in addition, the taxed country is a less efficient user of resources allocated to defence than the tax receiver this will assist a move to a Pareto optimum. The resources transferred by the tax will be used by the efficient country which means that the spillovers will be large, enabling the less efficient defence producer to release resources domestically for non-defence output—it will receive more defence cover and produce more private goods. In Sandler's model this last assumption requires that the constraint of identical production functions be relaxed so that one partner is more efficient in defence production than the other. It would also follow that taxing the relatively efficient producer and transferring to the less efficient producer would reduce that country's welfare.

Sandler confirms Olson & Zeckhauser's view that in equilibrium a 'large' country will provide all the defence of the members if the disparity in size is very great. By large Sandler specifically means size in resource endowment or GNP: 'Inasmuch as defense is desired for the purpose of protection of national income and lives, it seems reasonable that increases in national income would always enhance the consumption of the defence good because much more would be at stake' (Sandler 1975, p. 228). That more will be spent on defence absolutely as a country grows in size of GNP is not incompatible with a constant or declining D/GNP ratio. Sandler goes on to suggest that free riding by the smaller partner could mean no gains for the large partner from the alliance which might make it unstable, especially if there were negative spillins such as defence congestion imposed on the large country by having to cover the defence needs of a wider territory. To ameliorate this situation taxation transfers are suggested. These, of course, will not benefit the small country but the transaction might be possible if it is the price of the continuance of the alliance. However, the size of the transfer would be negotiable and would depend on how much each partner wanted the alliance to continue.

A recent contribution by Todd Sandler to alliance economics (Sandler 1977) approaches the transfer payment policy from another direction, by providing an alternative theory of alliance which uses the idea of defence goods being either pure or impure (partial) public goods. A defence good is exclusively for deterrence when 'the sole purpose is to convey a credible threat of retaliation on behalf of the alliance' and exclusively for protection when the weapons are used 'to shelter, retard, repel or forewarn against an attack' (Sandler 1977, p. 445). A third class of weapons exist which combine both categories of deterrence and protection, these are known as mixed defence weapons (MWs).

Deterrence weapons (DWs) are pure public goods because they are non-rival and non-exclusive and the traditional economic theory of alliance has been concerned mainly with these types of weapons. Protection Weapons (PWs) are usually impure or partial public goods due to 'elements of rivalry and exclusion embodied in the good's technology' (p. 446). Deterrence is indivisible because non-attack benefits everybody but protection is divisible because the probability of survival once an attack takes place (deterrence breaks down) is not equal for all citizens and all territories in the alliance. Protection forces are subject to what Mancur Olson describes as *thinning;* the more territory to be protected the thinner the protection provided by a given quantity of PWs.

A military alliance such as NATO consists of both DWs and PWs. In the case of DWs – those weapons exclusively concerned with deterrence – their deployment is less important than the commitment to use them. As for *PW*s, deployment is as crucial as commitment. There is considerable room for negotiation in the deployment of *PW*s among the member states of NATO and for national commitment of *PW*s to the alliance. Allocating *PW*s for alliance objectives contributes to thinning for national objectives – e.g. most of the Royal Air Force is committed to Germany at some cost to air defence in Britain. An increase in thinning reduces utility for the ally and thinning is related to both the total quantity of defence (X) provided by the alliance and total usage by the allies:

$$\left(\sum_{i=1}^{n} x^i \right)$$

In NATO there is pressure both to concentrate defence forces of the alliance (e.g. in Germany on the central front) and to raise national contributions to defence (e.g. pressure from NATO on Britain to restore the 1975–7 defence cuts).

Sandler concludes that alliances that are largely protective in nature are more likely to share burdens equitably because members must reveal their preferences for utilisation, and because thinning costs are more visible for specific deployments of *PW*s. Allies pressurising for given deployments of *PW*s, and given contributions of *PW*s from other allies, can in principle be charged user fees. This is in contrast to purely deterrent alliances where benefits from deterrence are indivisible.

This enables Sandler to specify a model for an alliance consisting of both *DW*s and *PW*s by hypothesising a general defence good (q) yielding a private good output (R), a purely public output (z) and an impurely public output (X). The optimal membership size and pricing conditions for the impurely public joint product are such that an additional member should be allowed into the alliance if the total benefits received by the member are greater than the thinning costs levied on the allies by the entrant's utilisation of the alliance defence, and the price or user fee of additional defence is equal to the sum of the thinning costs. Optimal provision of defence in an alliance with pure, impure and private outputs is given by:

$$MB_R^i + \sum_{i=1}^{n} MBT^i + \sum_{i=1}^{n} MB_z^i = MC_q$$

The marginal benefits of the private good output involve only the ally which receives them, the marginal benefits of deterrence must be summed over all the allies and the marginal benefits of protection (a reduction in thinning when the joint product impure public good is increased by decreasing the usage or increasing the quantity of PWs in the alliance) must also be summed across the alliance. The optimum is found when the sum of these benefits is equated to the marginal cost of providing the general defence good, q (p. 454).

Since both private benefits and thinning costs can be adjusted or withheld (an ally can refuse to deploy PWs to suit an ally unless reciprocal effort is made in defence provision) free-rider behaviour can be influenced, which is less likely in the purely deterrent model of alliances. Defence preferences will be revealed in deployment and user programmes for PWs where they might not be for DWs and the optimum can be approached using user fees or transfers between allies. This must introduce into alliance burden-sharing discussions a greater prospect of equitable burden sharing for that portion of the alliance defence output that consists of PWs and MWs such as in NATO. Britain, for instance, provides a substantial defence output of PWs and MWs, and deploys them largely in Germany. On this analysis it could (should) charge user fees for doing so.

The transfer problem

A cost-sharing scheme which involved transfers between members would not be without its economic problems, in particular the 'transfer problem' has to be faced. This arises because the movement of tax transfers between two countries, as proposed in the Sandler model, would have a counterpart in the movement of real resources between them. These real resources are a real cost to the donor country because they reduce the amount of real resources available for domestic use and they are a real benefit to the recipient country because they supplement its own domestic resources.

The donor country will experience at least one burden in the loss of the use of the foregone transferred resources. It might experience another burden in the balance of payments effects of the transfer. The donor must achieve an excess of exports over imports to effect the transfer and the recipient must accept an import surplus. This will not be without its effects on the exchange rates and the parties may be unable to manage the transfer without damaging other economic objectives (Johnson 1958; Hawkins 1970).

The economics involved can be illustrated by the use of standard text-book identities. Where Y is the domestic production of goods and services, M is imports, X is exports, C is consumption, G is government (including defence) and I is investment, the economy can be represented by:

$$Y + M = C + I + G + X$$

which in words states simply that domestic production plus imports are equal to (i.e. available for use as) consumption, investment, government and exports. In order to effect the transfer domestic use of available resources $(C + I + G)$ must permit the trade balance $(X - M)$ to be in surplus:

$$Y - (C + I + G) = X - M$$

The country concerned can bring this about by reducing domestic consumption of available resources through taxation or through permitting the terms of trade to depreciate its currency, thus raising import prices (reducing domestic real incomes) relative to export prices.

In the case of the recipient the transfer will be effected if there is an import surplus:

$$M - X = (C + I + G) - Y$$

Domestic consumption of resources in all uses will exceed domestic production (Y) by the import surplus, i.e. the transferred resources from the donor.

In the case of transfers between members for defence purposes of the alliance there are certain distinctive features of this type of transaction compared to the normal subjects of transfer-problem discussions, such as the cases of foreign aid and reparations from defeated enemies. First of all the transaction is between governments at one level but between the tax payers of one country (the donors) and the public expenditure sector of the other country (the recipient) on another. At the same time the taxpayers are receiving something they value—security—for the resources they sacrifice and the recipients are providing military services for what they are receiving. Both parties to the transaction are gaining through the public-good nature of alliance defence. Which partner does what will be decided by comparative advantage and which of them pays for it to be done will be decided by ability to pay (perhaps modified by benefit considerations).

Can the resources be raised in the donor country and successfully transferred to the recipient? Apart from the political considerations there are economic ones. If the donor country has full employment of domestic resources it might face some difficulty in arranging the transfer (deflation) but this might be more manageable if it can meet its obligations by the transfer of physical output and services to the recipient. In this case the government purchases the required goods and services from its own citizens and hands them over to the recipient. This would involve G rising at the expense of C and I, or a shift from private resource usage to public resource usage. There would be no balance of payments problems in this action. If the donor made foreign exchange available to the recipient the mechanism of the transfer could be more complex but nevertheless amounts to something similar. Foreign exchange is a claim on a country's resources which can be made now or in the future. If the recipient spends the foreign exchange in third party countries it transfers those claims to others who may or may not make them immediately. The chain may be a long one or a short one—real resources flow from the third party country to the recipient and from the donor to the third party. If the resources are not available from the donor it will experience pressure on its exchange rate and perhaps some inflation domestically.

The donor country may hold substantial foreign exchange reserves from its normal commercial transactions, i.e. it may hold claims against foreign countries among which might be the potential recipient in the alliance. In this case it would transfer its claims on third parties to the recipient or reduce its claims on the recipient. If the recipient was in substantial deficit arising from its normal commercial transactions this would ease pressure on its exchange rate. It might even cover its deficit. In this case the transfer is taking the form of the surplus of imports over exports of the recipient country, some part of which originates directly with the donor and the rest indirectly through third parties. If the transfer was in physical goods and services and not foreign exchange the recipient government would reduce its own G and increase C and I, or shift resources from public to private usage. Again, this is unlikely to have balance of payments implications, particularly if the recipient country also happened to be engaged in military services within the donor country. This was much of the rationale behind the German offset agreements to cover American and British expenses from military services in Germany.

Another difference between transfers within an alliance and foreign aid is the non-repayable status of such transfers. There is no question of the donor expecting a return from the transfer of a financial nature. The resources do not have to find some use which generates an income stream in the recipient country in the way in which investment aid is expected to provide some development potential. The donor is expecting a contribution from the recipient of military services to the alliance and this provides a welcome check on the efficient use of the resources—they must at least meet international alliance standards of effectiveness.

However, much of this assumes away the political problems of inducing one country's tax payers to cover the costs of another country's military provision. Military aid is, of course, not unknown. It regularly occurs on a substantial scale throughout the world. But substantial transfers within an alliance of the type suggested here are something new, particularly as it would appear on ability-to-pay criteria that some of the smaller GNP countries would be contributing to the transfer as well as some of the larger GNP countries. Also, the economic problems of members are themselves a highly sensitive subject, and dramatic change of this kind could not but have an unsettling effect on exchange rates which could have repercussions on domestic political balances.

Comparative advantage and alliance efficiency

Hoag (1957) in one of the earlier, and incidentally most perceptive, contributions to alliance economics, set out the options which an alliance such as NATO could choose from in a quest for alliance efficiency and equity in burden sharing. Over twenty years later the options remain much the same and a review of them is instructive in how far, or how little, the debate has moved in the meantime (see Hartley & Peacock 1978).

The resource allocation problem within an alliance is similar to the allocative problem in international production: 'resources should nowhere be employed to produce something directly when those same resources could produce more of it indirectly; that is, produce a different product for more of the initial alternative product' (Hoag 1957, p. 528). This is the classic argument for free trade. Its relevance for alliance economics lies in the public good nature of alliance output, the ability to substitute military output between partners, the relative comparative advantage of members in respect of military outputs, and the assumption that the alliance members seek the same or more defence at less cost.

The extreme solution is to pool all defence resources in the alliance and run the alliance from the centre. In NATO's case this would be impossible because the alliance exists to preserve national sovereignties, not remove them. The middle-ground solution is to allocate defence tasks to members on the principle of comparative advantage, with members specialising in those activities where they have a comparative advantage over other members. One guide to comparative advantage would be the composition of each member's present military effort on the assumption that in the main a country will be allocating most resources to those elements of total defence in which it has discovered national advantages already. The other guide would come from military evaluation of efforts contributed to the alliance. Delicate political issues could arise in such an evaluation because essentially the members will be deciding whether a particular national force, say, a navy or army corps, could be a substitute for other members' contributions—is the British Army on the Rhine a perfect substitute for the American or German armies? If not, by how much is it less or more militarily effective?

In Tables 7.1 and 7.2 the manpower composition of the NATO defence forces and the major weapon systems associated with each force are shown. America has an almost three-way split between the army, navy and air force demonstrating its all-round capability. Germany, France and Britain have much in common in weapon systems but differ in their composition of forces. Germany has next to no navy and a heavy preponderance of ground forces, while Britain and France are more similarly balanced between the three forces. Turkey, Greece, the Netherlands, Belgium, Denmark and Portugal (in 1976) predominantly specialised in the ground-force role.

According to the discussions in Chapter Five Britain was grossly over-subscribed in its defence contribution on an ability-to-pay formula. If this was to be adjusted it could mean

Table 7.1 Composition of armed forces: NATO members

Member Country	Numbers (ooo's)			Percentage		
	Army	Navy	Air	Army	Navy	Air
1 America	789	728	571	38	35	27
2 Turkey	375	43	47	80	9	10
3 Germany	341	38	110	70	8	22
4 France	330	68	103	66	14	21
5 Italy	218	42	70	66	13	21
6 Britain	175.3	76.7	87.2	52	23	26
7 Greece	160	17.5	22.5	80	9	11
8 Netherlands	75	17	17.7	68	15	16
9 Belgium	62.1	4.2	19.4	72	5	23
10 Portugal	36	12.8	10	61	22	17
11 Canada	28.5	13.5	36.6	36	17	46
12 Denmark	21.8	5.8	7.1	63	17	20
13 Norway	20	9	10	51	23	26
14 Luxembourg	0.6	—	—	100	—	—

Sources: numbers: IISS 1977–8; Table 3, p. 84, extracted and rearranged

Table 7.2 Inventory of major weapon systems, NATO members, 1976 (ranked by size of defence budgets)

Country	MBT	LT	APCs	PGWs	Hel. army	Major combat surface ships	Light combat surface ships	Sub-marines	MCMs	Combat naval aircraft	Combat naval Hel.	Combat aircraft air force	Hel. air force
America	6 700	5 375	22 000	905●	8 000	175	69	78	3	1 565‡	426‡	3 400	422
Germany	1 400	2 437	7 736	1 516	550	17	56	24	57	139	63	509	117
France	1 060	1 120	1 392	92●	552	53	32	21	38	111	70	557	197
Britain	910	271	5 395	101●	384	75	23	31	43	26	129	550	71†
Italy	1 500		4 030	172●	872	19	18	8	44		56	336	130
Netherlands	810		2 000	106●	90	15	46	6	37	23	19	162	
Canada		255	1 122	103†		21	6	3				210	
Turkey	4 450	604	1 650	18†	168	14		14	25	10	15	319	30
Belgium	186		1 390†	113†	74	2	8		29		4	144	8
Norway			nd	nd	nd	5	13	15	10			145	42
Denmark	308		698	nd	12	7	46	6	8	8		116	8
Greece	1 170		1 130	nd	72	15	13	6	14		5	235	38
Portugal	115		40†			7	28	3	7			52	46

Source: IISS 1977–8, extracted from tables

● for 1973
† known figure only, actual total exceeds this quantity
‡ includes Marine Corps inventory
nd no details available, though country known to possess these weapons

Note: MBT = main battle tank; LT = medium and light tanks; APCs = armoured fighting vehicles, armoured personnel carriers; PGWs = precision guided weapons; Hel. = helicopter; MCMs = mines counter measures vessels; Major combat surface ships include all combat vessels from frigate upwards; submarines include nuclear powered boats.

one of two options: either Britain's real contribution is taken over by some other member or members, or Britain continues with its contribution but is paid to do so by the alliance. If the former were decided upon the redistribution of Britain's defence tasks among the members would be a formidable exercise: Which country (countries) would be best placed to do this as effectively as Britain does at the moment? The transition costs would be bound to be high if alliance effectiveness was not to be damaged. It might not only be more sensible from a military and alliance point of view to encourage Britain to continue with its current contributions but advantageous to the alliance to provide the resources for Britain to expand in some areas where its comparative advantages are substantial.

In Table 5.4 the proposed redistribution among the members led to Britain reducing its own defence budget in US dollars from $11 billion to $5 billion and the increases in other members' budgets were sufficient not only to cover this reduction but also the entire defence budgets of the very poorest of the NATO members (Italy, Turkey, Greece, Portugal). Of course, Table 5.4 is not to be understood in a prescriptive sense but only in illustration of the application of a principle. It merely demonstrates the possibilities.

Identifying comparative advantages in military provision is only a partial solution to the problem of alliance efficiency. It also creates the possibility of a perverse reaction by members. Budgeteers the world over respond to the same stimuli. They all have demands upon them in excess of their resources and they are likely to treat international transfers as a windfall gain and adjust their behaviour accordingly. Britain provides an example of this in respect of the Regional Fund of the European Economic Community. The fund is meant to *supplement* national efforts at regional development. In the British case, much to the annoyance of their partners, funds emanating from the EEC for these purposes have been regarded as substitutes for national funds rather than supplements and national efforts have been reduced by exactly the same amount as have been supplied by the EEC. In other words the EEC is not adding to Britain's national efforts at regional development but merely replacing them. There is no reason to believe that HM Treasury would react any differently in a NATO-managed transfer scheme. As Hoag put it (1957, p. 524) the incentive effect of this kind of windfall on the budgeteer would most likely be for him to tell his NATO counterparts: 'You wish us to provide X because we are especially good at it? Splendid; our military leaders quite agree. Unfortunately, it lies beyond our means.'

In the real world there is likely to be a dispute over how far a poorer member's economic ranking is due to its wilful inability to alter its economic policies or behaviour rather than some historical or endowment disadvantage. This will ensure that any discussions held with a view to some transfer scheme will involve argument as well as bargaining.

There may be an assumption that there are gains from forming an alliance, but the gains may be unidentifiable let alone asymmetrical. In both cases this makes the allocative process difficult. But not knowing how far to go may be less important than agreeing on which direction to go in. If the alliance can agree that in general it is preferable from an efficiency point of view to encourage specialisation among members it can adopt a policy of removing barriers to specialisation where they exist. Complementary to this policy the alliance may favour the encouragement of standardisation in the fields of equipment, communications and methods or, as a first step, compatability between national defence operations. NATO has in the past struggled to achieve these objectives and is making some progress, but as with any change in direction there are costs as well as benefits. A 'second best' solution may not be better than nothing if a 'first best' solution is unobtainable (Lipsey & Lancaster 1956–7).

The result of imprecision in defining the gains and who gets them in the alliance is almost fatal to the policy prescription of searching for and promoting them. The alliance is a forum, not an instrument of collective will. 'As a result,' writes Hoag (1957, p. 529), 'a necessary condition for a balanced collective force is transformed from the inadmissible form—military capabilities everywhere provided where cheapest in the alliance—to military capabilities nowhere provided more expensively than genuine lack of substitutability of external performance warrants.' Attempts to specify 'genuine lack of substitutability' where national issues are at stake are likely to flounder. Is the German main battle tank a perfect substitute for the British one? Should the British equip themselves (at German expense) with German tanks for use by their forces in Germany? What are the employment consequences in the British defence industries of such a decision? Would there be a shift out of defence activities into non-defence activities in Britain (and the reverse in Germany) or a shift from employment into unemployment of British resources?

8

Summary and Conclusions

Readers who have worked their way through the book to this chapter will by now be well aware that the issues raised by burden sharing do not lead to simple solutions, or at least they have not so far in the history of NATO. This does not in any way discount the value of discussing burden sharing and attempting to find an agreed formula for redistributing the burden among the allies. The very willingness to discuss the matter at all is in itself an inducement to individual members to accept, on a voluntary basis, some new military tasks on behalf of the alliance which they may previously have left to others, perhaps out of ignorance of the real strains this was imposing on their neighbours. Such discussions may strengthen the alliance by the discovery of new forms of military co-operation. They may spur efforts to procure collaboration. A failure to discuss the issue could mean that the current distribution of the defence burden was perfectly satisfactory to the members because it met the tests of equity and effectiveness. Moreover, it would suggest that the politics of the current distribution are more important than the economics. But with international co-operation increasing in and through organisations which have, or derive, cost-sharing formulae using explicit criteria it is likely that the pressure to continue the discussion on burden sharing in NATO will increase rather than diminish. However, it is best to cultivate modest expectations for change in this area.

Britain is one of the major military powers in NATO and there is no doubt that the economic strains of the past twenty years are having their effect on the presentation of options which government and opposition are being forced to consider. It would be wrong and misleading to see a cause-and-effect relationship between Britain's economic difficulties and current debates about defence. Some participants in the debate would hold the same views whether Britain was booming or bust: they are anti-NATO in principle (some, a minority, are simply pro-Soviet) and believe NATO contributes to European tension rather than lowers it. Thirty years of peace in Europe does nothing to convince them of NATO's success. They are increasingly intimidated by the possibility of war breaking out by accident or by the provocation of Russia. This point of view can be seen succinctly in the report of the Labour Party defence study group (Labour Party 1977).

The British Government has also contributed to the debate in recent years. To some extent it has presented several rather contradictory views. Ministry of Defence White Papers (MOD 1975, 1976, 1977, 1978) have taken the format of one part outlining how serious the growing WARPAC threat is becoming from its persistent military build-up, followed by a second part which outlines why the defence budget has to be reduced. The views outlined in the 1975 *Statement on the Defence Estimates* (MOD 1975) expressed the official view admirably:

> Throughout the post-war period Britain's economic perfor-
> mance has lagged behind that of her major European Allies.
> For many years our annual average growth rate has been little
> more than half that achieved by France and the Federal
> Republic of Germany. For this reason and because our
> economic situation is now more serious than at any time over
> the last 25 years, the Government decided that resources must
> be released for investment and improving the balance of
> payments. These should be the first calls on our resources in
> solving economic problems. The defence programme, with its
> considerable demands on skilled manpower and industry,
> should play its part in this process: and the burden of defence
> expenditure should be brought more into line with that of our
> major European Allies. Planned British defence expenditure in
> 1974 was estimated at 5·8 per cent of GNP on NATO defini-
> tion, while that of France was 3·8 per cent, and of the Federal
> Republic of Germany 4·1 per cent (or 4·9 per cent including
> Berlin Aid).

The Government set itself a target of reducing the D/GNP ratio to 4·5 per cent by 1984 and through this of diverting £4700 million from defence in that time period, ostensibly into investment and the balance of payments problem. It was aiming to do this while safeguarding the 'essential security interests of Britain and her Allies' (MOD 1975, p. 2). The Allies apparently were unimpressed by this assurance and the most strenuous, and eventually successful, pressure was exerted through NATO on the British Government to reverse or restrain this policy and in 1978 some restorations were made to the projected defence budget (MOD 1978).

We do not have to accept the programme laid out in the Labour Party's *Sense About Defence* (Labour Party 1977) to be aware that the burden on Britain of sustaining its major contribution to NATO is inequitable on ability-to-pay criteria. The relative position of Britain's economy has certainly declined since NATO was formed in 1949. In per capita terms it has fallen well behind most of its European partners and especially the Big Two, France and Germany. The fact that Britain contributes so much is a testimony to its commitment. Nor do we have to believe that its defence contribution is a cause of its economic difficulties (Smith 1977), or, as other left-wing researchers argue, that defence expenditure is a prop to avert economic crisis (Kidron 1970). (These and similar views are criticised in Kennedy 1975, and Hartley & McLean 1978.)

The case for burden sharing can be made as part of a programme to maintain current British defence efforts, on comparative advantage grounds, or increase them as well as reduce them. The issue in burden sharing is who provides the resources?

Summary

Voluntary provision of public goods is likely to lead to suboptimal provision because of the individual free-rider problem. In alliances this appears in the form of disproportionate D/GNP ratios related to the relative willingness of members to provide for defence, given the existence of the alliance and the knowledge that some members are prepared, or have been in the past, to undertake greater commitments either because of their greater threat perception or because they are allowed a greater degree of political influence from doing so. It is also possible that D/GNP ratios may diverge over time due to greater economic efficiency and more rapid growth by some members.

The economic theory of alliances suggested that disproportionate D/GNP ratios, if associated with the size of the GNP, and if the size of the GNP was related to capacity to pay, would be equitable on cost-sharing grounds. Empirical support for the relationship between D/GNP and absolute size of the GNP was not found to be significant for NATO nor was it accepted that the size of the GNP was an unambiguous measure of ability-to-pay. Circumstance as well as income would have to be considered and this led to the use of per capita income as a more reliable guide. Benefit criteria, while found to be analytically attractive, were not regarded as operational in this case due to the inability to decide on the gainers or to compel them to reveal their preferences. Alliances produce deterrence and deterrence is indivisible (but see Sandler 1977).

The reworking of De Strihou's method confirmed and strengthened his earlier results. If America's D/GNP ratio is taken as a standard for the richer NATO members it is clear that in 1975 Britain's D/GNP ratio was considerably in excess of its appropriate ratio if the British progressivity schedule was acceptable (which it clearly must be to the British at least). This suggested that defence expenditures of the other NATO allies ought, on distributional grounds, to be increased and Britain's reduced (and the poorer members' defence expenditures reduced to zero).

The economics of tax transfers applied to an alliance (Sandler's model) showed that welfare of the alliance members could be improved by (a) joining an alliance and (b) engaging in tax transfers to the most efficient military producer. This gave a theoretical justification for a tax transfer scheme for NATO. It did not follow that such a scheme would solve the current inequity within NATO: the efficiency criteria may suggest a reverse tax transfer flow to the equity criteria, e.g. Britain may pay its partners to produce defence on efficiency grounds but receive payments on equity grounds.

There are other formidable obstacles to the tax transfer scheme. There is the transfer problem itself which highlights resistance in both countries to permitting the transfer to take place because of its side effects. There is also the problem of identifying comparative advantage in the member countries in military specialisation. Military resources are not perfectly substitutable between countries and there may be substantial political barriers to specialisation even if they were. The alliance output may be a partial public good and national defence provision may of necessity be at variance with perfect alliance efficiency.

Conclusions

A frontal assault on the burden-sharing issue in NATO in respect of the main defence budgets of the members is extremely unlikely for the present. If one was to take place it would have to take account of some formidable problems.

From the discussions in this book it is at least clear that no single criterion is likely to emerge as *the* criterion for burden sharing. A mixture is more likely. The broad principles might be:

1. All members should contribute *something* to the common defence. This might be a fully equipped and trained military force or geographical access (as in the case of Iceland) in recognition of the benefit principle.
2. Members' overall contributions should take account of their capacity to pay. This can be estimated using *both* the absolute size of the GNP and per capita GNP.
3. No member's contribution should be permitted to get too far out of line, over a certain length of time, with the estimated capacity to pay. This allows for secular changes in relative economic growth.
4. The use of agreed formulae for allocating infrastructure and headquarters costs should be extended into as many marginal and minor programmes as possible. The data upon which allocations are made should be publicised within the alliance (as percentages if security con-

siderations are important in specific cases) in order to promote discussion on their comparability with the main budget allocations.

5. A modified version of the progressivity allocation discussed in this book should be developed in order to see what is involved in a tax transfer scheme, how it would notionally be distributed and to whom. If the British tax progressivity schedule is regarded as too steep then other schedules can be tried including shadow ones. If discussion is encouraged the political processes will concentrate on the practicalities of adopting alternative schemes rather than ignoring, or condemning, the issue on principle.

6. If such a scheme were proposed it should be administered by the NATO secretariat from a public-records point of view but managed bilaterally between the members concerned.

7. As much effort as possible should go into devising bilateral transfers on as imaginative a scale as possible especially on identifiable projects. The earlier offset agreements and their adaptations provide useful experience. With identifiable projects it is possible for the donor to measure the quality standards of the recipient's efforts which might not be the case if the transfer simply went into the total budget.

8. Neither the donor nor the recipient status of a member should have any formal recognition in the NATO political structure.

The pressure for some resolution of the burden-sharing issue will come to fruition if, and only if, the members wish it. Unilateral action is always a possibility but, as the British example shows, political considerations tend to over-ride temporary economic ones particularly if, as was the case, the security considerations begin to emerge as an even more serious threat to the status quo than perceptions of economic interest. If a member engages in unilateral action—the ultimate sanction is withdrawal—it has to be sure that the result will improve the situation, not worsen it. The best way to shed some of Britain's defence burden is to negotiate with its allies. This could usefully be supplemented with a determined assault on its chronic economic problems—faster growth in real terms would reduce the D/GNP ratio more safely than panic defence cuts.

Western Europe is one of the world's richest economic zones in per capita GNP and absolute GNP. It ought to be able to afford a secure defence. As every economist knows it is a matter of making choices. Informed choice has a head start over ignorance. That is where the economics of military alliance will make a modest contribution.

Bibliography

Allan, Charles M. (1971): *The Theory of Taxation*, Penguin Modern Economics, Harmondsworth

Ashcroft, Geoffrey (1969): *Military Logistics Systems in NATO: the goal of integration. Part 1: economic aspects,* International Institute for Strategic Studies, Adelphi paper no. 67, London, November

Beer, F. A. (1972): *The Political Economy of Alliances: benefits, costs, and institutions in NATO*, Sage Professional Papers in International Studies, Sage, Beverly Hills

Bendall, David (1963): 'Burden Sharing in NATO', *NATO Letter*, Brussels, September

Benoit, Emile (1973): *Defense and Economic Growth in Developing Countries*, Lexington Books, D. C. Heath, Lexington, Mass.

Benoit, Emile & Lubell, H. (1960): 'World Defence Expenditures', *Journal of Peace Research*, 2, pp. 97–113

Bowen, H. R. (1948): *Towards Social Economy*, Reinhart, New York

Breton, A. (1970): 'Public Goods and the Stability of Federalism', *Kyklos*, 23, pp. 882–902

Brodie, Bernard (1963): 'What Price Conventional Capabilities in Europe?', *The Reporter*, 28, 23 May, p. 27

Buchanan, James M. (1965): 'An Economic Theory of Clubs', *Economica*, 32, February, pp. 1–14

Buchanan, James M. (1968): *The Demand and Supply of Public Goods*, Rand McNally, Chicago

Coase, R. H. (1974): 'The Lighthouse in Economics', *Journal of Law and Economics*, 17, October, pp. 357–76

Cockle, P. (1977): *Observations on the Proposal to Align UK Defence Expenditures with the Average Spent on Defence by the FRG, Italy and France,* Labour Party Defence Study Group, Labour Party, London

Cockle, P. (1978): 'Analysing Soviet Defence Spending: the debate in perspective', *Survival*, 20, no. 5, Sept.-Oct., pp. 209–19

David, Paul A. (1972) 'Just How Misleading are Official Exchange Rate Conversions?', *Economic Journal*, 82, September, no. 327, pp. 979–90

De Strihou, Jacques M. V. Y. (1968): 'Sharing the Defence Burden

Among Western Allies', *Yale Economic Essays,* **8,** Spring, pp. 261–320

De Strihou, Jacques M. V. Y. (1968): 'Sharing the Defence Burden Among Western Allies', *Review of Economics and Statistics,* **50,** pp. 527–36

Edgeworth, F. Y. (1897): *Papers Relating to Political Economy,* Macmillan, London (1925), 2 vols

FAO (Food and Agriculture Organisation) (1975): *Report of the Expert Consultation on Cereal Stock Policies Relating to World Food Security to the Committee on Commodity Problems,* Rome, February

Gilbert and Associates (1957): *Comparative National Products and Price Levels,* OEEC, Paris

Gilbert, M. & Kravis, I. B. (1954): *An International Comparison of National Products and the Purchasing Power of Currencies,* OEEC, Paris

Hackel, Erwin (1970): *Military Manpower and Political Purpose,* IISS, Adelphi Paper no. 72, London, December

Hartley, Keith and McLean, Pat (1978): 'Military Expenditure and Capitalism: a comment', *Cambridge Journal of Economics,* **2,** no. 3, September, pp. 287–92

Hartley, Keith and Peacock, Alan (1978): 'Combined Defence and International Economic Co-operation', *World Economy,* **1,** no. 3, June, pp. 327–39

Hawkins, E. K. (1970): *The Principles of Development Aid,* Penguin Modern Economics, Harmondsworth

Hoag, Malcolm W. (1957): 'Economic Problems of Alliances', *Journal of Political Economy,* **65,** no. 6, pp. 522–35

Hoffman, Walther G. (1969): 'The Share of Defence Expenditures in Gross National Product (GNP): an international and diachronic comparison', *German Economic Review,* **7,** part 4, pp. 294–307

IISS (International Institute for Strategic Studies) (annual: 1972, 1973, 1974, 1975, 1976, 1977, 1978): *The Military Balance,* London

Johansen, Leif (1965): *Public Economics,* North Holland, Amsterdam

Johnson, Harry G. (1958): 'Towards a General Theory of the Balance of Payments', in his *International Trade and Economic Growth: studies in pure theory,* Allen & Unwin, London, pp. 153–68

Kennedy, Gavin (1975): *The Economics of Defence,* Faber and Faber, London

Kennedy, Gavin (1978): *A Note on the Economic Theory of Alliances,* Discussion Paper, 78/3, Department of Economics, University of Strathclyde, Glasgow

Kidron, Michael (1970): *Western Capitalism Since the War,* Penguin, Harmondsworth

Knorr, Klaus (1961): *Notes on a Theory of Alliances*, unpublished MS, Centre of International Studies, Princeton University

Knorr, Klaus (1970): *Military Power and Potential*, Lexington Books, D. C. Heath, Mass.

Kravis, Irving B., Kenessy, Zoltan, Heston, Allan & Summers, Robert (1975): *A System of International Comparisons of Gross Product and Purchasing Power*, John Hopkins and World Bank, Baltimore

Kravis, Irving B. & Davenport, M. W. S. (1963): 'The Political Arithmetic of International Burden Sharing', *Journal of Political Economy*, **71**, no. 4, August, pp. 309–30

Labour Party (1977): *Sense About Defence: the report of the Labour Party Defence Study Group*, introduced by Ian Mikardo, Quest, London

Lincoln, Gordon (1956): 'Economic Aspects of Coalition Diplomacy: the NATO experience', *International Organisation*, **4**, November

Lindhal, Erik (1919): 'Just Taxation—A Positive Solution' in Musgrave & Peacock (1958) pp. 168–76

Lipsey, Richard G. & Lancaster, K. (1956–7): 'The General Theory of the Second Best', *Review of Economic Studies*, **24**, pp. 11–32

Loehr, W. (1973): 'Collective Goods and International Co-operation: comments', *International Organisation*, **27**, Summer, pp. 421–30

McGuire, M. C. & Aaron, H. (1969): 'Efficiency and Equity in the Optimal Supply of a Public Good', *Review of Economics and Statistics*, **51**, no. 1, pp. 31–9

Margolis, J. (1954): 'A Comment on the Pure Theory of Public Expenditures', *Review of Economics and Statistics*, **37**, pp. 347–9

Mason, Edward S. (1963): 'The Equitable Sharing of Military and Economic Aid Burdens', *Proceedings of the Academy of Political Science*, **27**, May, pp. 256–69

Meade, James E. (1973): *The Theory of Economic Externalities and the Control of Environmental Pollution and Other Social Costs*, Sijthoff, Leiden

Mill, John Stuart (1848): *Principles of Political Economy with Some of their Applications to Social Philosophy*, London

MOD (Ministry of Defence) (annual: 1975, 1976, 1977, 1978): *Statement on the Defence Estimates*, HMSO, London, Cmnd 5976, 6432, 6735, 7099

Morse, Edward L. (1976): 'The Bargaining Structure of NATO: multi-issue negotiations in an inter-dependent world', in Zartman, I. William: *The 50% Solution*, Anchor, New York, pp. 66–97

Morton, Kathryn & Tulloch, Peter (1977): *Trade and Developing Countries*, Croom Helm and Overseas Development Institute, London

Musgrave, Richard A. (1959): *The Theory of Public Finance*, McGraw-Hill Kogakusha, Tokyo

Musgrave, Richard A. (1966): 'Provision for Social Goods' in Margolis, J. and Guitton, H. (eds) *Public Economics,* International Economics Association, London

Musgrave, Richard A. (1969): *Fiscal Systems,* Yale University Press, Newhaven, Conn.

Musgrave, Richard & Musgrave, Peggy (1976): *Public Finance in Theory and Practice,* McGraw-Hill Kogakusha, Tokyo (2nd ed.)

Musgrave, Richard & Peacock, Alan (1958): *Classics in the Theory of Public Finance,* Macmillan, London

Myers, Denys P. (1935): *Handbook of the League of Nations,* New York

NATO (North Atlantic Treaty Organisation) (1955): *NATO: the First Five Years,* Paris

NATO (1976a): *NATO Review,* February

NATO (1976): *NATO Facts and Figures,* Brussels

NATO (1978): *NATO Handbook,* Brussels

Nichols, Calvin J. (1961): *Financing the United Nations: problems and prospects,* Centre for International Studies, MIT, Cambridge, Mass.

Olson, Mancur (1965): *The Logic of Collective Action: public goods and the theory of groups,* Harvard University Press, Harvard, Mass.

Olson, Mancur (1967): 'Collective Goods, Comparative Advantage, and Alliance Efficiency' in McKean, Roland N. (ed.): *Issues in Defense Economics,* National Bureau of Economic Research, New York, 1967, pp. 25–48

Olson, Mancur (1971): 'Increasing the Incentives for International Co-operation', *International Organisation,* **25,** Autumn, pp. 866–74

Olson, Mancur & Zeckhauser, Richard (1968): 'An Economic Theory of Alliances', *Reveiw of Economics and Statistics,* **48,** August, pp. 266–74

Padelford, Norman J. (1963): 'Financial Crisis and the Future of the United Nations', *World Politics,* **17,** July

Peacock, Alan (1972): 'The Public Finance of Inter-Allied Defence Provision', in *Essays in Honour of Antonia de Viti de Marco,* Caccuci Editore, Bari

Peston, Maurice (1972): *Public Goods and the Public Sector,* Macmillan Studies in Economics, Macmillan, London

Pincus, John A. (1962): *Sharing the Costs of Military Alliance and Economic Aid,* Rand, Santa Monica, RM-3249

Pincus, John A. (1965): *Economic Aid and International Cost Sharing,* Johns Hopkins, Baltimore

Pryor, Frederic L. (1968): *Public Expenditures in Communist and Capitalist Nations,* Allen & Unwin, London

Reinsch, Paul S. (1916): *Public International Unions,* World Peace Foundation

Rosenstein–Rodan, P. N. (1961): 'International Aid for Underdeveloped Countries', *Review of Economics and Statistics*, **41**, May, pp. 107–38

Roth, Gabriel (1967): *Paying For Roads: the economics of traffic congestion*, Penguin, Harmondsworth

Russett, Bruce M. (1964): 'Measures of Military Effort', *American Behavioural Scientist*, February, pp. 26–9

Russett, Bruce M. (1969): 'Who Pays for Defense?', *American Political Science Review*, **63**, June, pp. 412–26

Russett, Bruce M. (1970): *What Price Vigilance? The Burdens of National Defense*, Yale University Press, London

Russett, Bruce M. and Sullivan, John (1969): 'Collective Goods and International Organisations', *International Organisation*, **25**, Autumn, pp. 845–65

Samuelson, Paul A. (1954): 'The Pure Theory of Public Expenditure' *Review of Economics and Statistics*, **36**, no. 4, pp. 387–9

Samuelson, Paul A (1955): 'Diagrammatic Exposition of a Theory of Public Expenditure', *Review of Economics and Statistics*, **37**, pp. 350–6

Sandler, Todd (1975): 'The Economic Theory of Alliances: realigned' in Liske C., Loehr W. & McCamant J. (eds): *Comparative Public Policy: issues, theories and methods*, Sage and John Wiley, New York, pp. 223–39

Sandler, Todd (1977): 'Impurity of Defense: an application to the economics of alliances', *Kyklos*, **30**, Fasc. 3, pp. 443–60

Sandler, Todd and Cauley, Jon (1975): 'On the Economic Theory of Alliances', *Journal of Conflict Resolution*, **19**, June, pp. 330–48

Schelling, Thomas C. (1955): *International Cost Sharing Arrangements*, Essays In International Finance, no. 24, Princeton

Sertoli, Giandomenico (1961): 'The Structure and Financial Activities of European Regional Communities', *Law and Contemporary Problems*, **26**, Summer

Singer, David J. (1959): 'The Finances of the League of Nations', *International Organisation*, **13**, Winter, 1959

Singer, David J. (1961): *Financing International Organisation: the United Nations budget process*, Nijhoff, The Hague

Sloss, Leon (1975): *NATO Reform: prospects and priorities*, Washington Paper no. 30, Sage, London

Smith, Adam (1776): *An Inquiry into the Nature and Causes of the Wealth of Nations*, London

Smith, R. P. (1977): 'Military Expenditures and Capitalism', *Cambridge Journal of Economics*, **1**, no. 1, March, pp. 61–76

Stoessinger, John G. and Associates (1964): *Financing the United Nations System*, Brookings, Washington

Sumberg, T. A. (1946): 'Financing International Institutions', *Social Research,* September, pp. 276–306

Szawlowski, R. (1961): 'The Budget and the Budgetary Law of an International Governmental Organisation', *Public Finance,* 3–4, pp. 343–65

UN (United Nations) (1961): *Official Records,* General Assembly, Sixteenth Session, Supplement no. 10, Doc A/4775, New York

UN (1974): 'The Declaration and Programme of Action on the Establishment of a New International Economic Order', *Official Records,* Sixth Special Session, Part II, Doc A/9556, May, New York

Vandermater E. (1967): *Common Funding in NATO,* Rand, Santa Monica, RM 5282PR

Väyrynen, Raimo (1976): 'The Theory of Collective Goods, Military Alliances and International Security', *International Social Science Journal,* 38, June, pp. 288–305

Wagner, R. Harrison (1975): 'National Defense as a Collective Good', in Liske, C., Loehr, W. & McCamant, J. (eds): *Comparative Public Policy: issues, theories and methods,* Sage and John Wiley, New York, pp. 199–221

Warburton, Anne M. & Wood, John B. (n.d.): *Paying For NATO,* Friends of the Atlantic Union, London

World Bank (1977): *World Tables 1976,* Washington

Index